C000155017

Synergy Theatre Project in association with Theatre503 presents

THERE IS
A FIELD

Martin Askew

Commissioned by Synergy Theatre Project, *There Is A Field* was first presented by Synergy Theatre Project in association with Theatre503 on 20 February 2019 at Theatre503, London.

Cast

ABDULLAH / MARK	Sam Frenchum
SALEH	Archie Backhouse
AMINA	Roseanna Frascona
MAUREEN	Sarah Finigan
TONY	Fabrizio Santino

Creative Team

Director	Esther Baker
Designers	Katy McPhee and Patrick Bill
Lighting Designer	Tony Simpson
Assistant Director	Danielle Baker
Casting Director	Nadine Rennie CDG
Dramaturg	Neil Grutchfield
Production Manager	Steve Wald
Company Stage Manager	Katie Patrick
Stage Manager	Michael Smith
Assistant Stage Manager	Trey Foster

Please note that the text of the play which appears in this volume may be changed during the rehearsal process and appear in a slightly altered form in performance.

Supported by

Synergy Theatre Project

Synergy Theatre Project creates ground-breaking work which harnesses the energy, instincts and life experiences of those we work with – prisoners, ex-prisoners, young offenders and young people at risk of offending – gives them a voice and, in doing so, their dignity back. We inspire change by affecting feelings, attitudes and behaviour and provide practical opportunities which build a bridge from prison to social reintegration.

We are also concerned with the impact of our work on the public and use stories to humanise and provide new insights into the criminal justice system. Central to our approach is a commitment to artistic quality and empowerment of beneficiaries with the work taking place both in theatres and prisons and non-traditional venues, playing to diverse audiences and promoting mutual exchange between performers and audience to break down social barriers.

Staff
Artistic Director Esther Baker
General Manager Jennie McClure
New Writing Manager Neil Grutchfield
Learning & Engagement Manager (Adults) Denise Heard
Learning & Engagement Manager (Young People) Sinéad Emery
Learning & Engagement Assistant Karl Smith

Board of Trustees
Jules Carey
Paula Hamilton
Clíóna Roberts
Deborah Samuel
Jonathan Smith
Gaby Sumner
Catherine Thornborrow

Patron
Martin McDonagh

www.synergytheatreproject.co.uk

THEATRE 503

Theatre503 is the home of new writers and a launchpad for the artists who bring their words to life. We are pioneers in supporting new writers and a champion of their role in the theatre ecology. We find exceptional playwrights who will define the canon for the next generation. Learning and career development are at the core of what we do. We stage the work of more debut and emerging writers than any other theatre in the country. In the last year alone we staged 70 productions featuring 161 writers from short plays to full runs of superb drama and launching over 1,000 artists in the process. We passionately believe the most important element in a writer's development is to see their work developed through to a full production on stage, performed to the highest professional standard in front of an audience.

Over the last decade many first-time writers have gone on to establish a career in the industry thanks to the support of Theatre503: Tom Morton-Smith (Oppenheimer, RSC & West End), Anna Jordan (Bruntwood Prize Winner for Yen, Royal Exchange, Royal Court and Broadway), Vinay Patel (writer of the BAFTA winning Murdered By My Father), Katori Hall (Mountaintop, 503, West End & Broadway – winner of 503's first Olivier Award) and Jon Brittain (Rotterdam – winner of our second Olivier Award in 2017).

Theatre503 Team
Artistic Director Lisa Spirling
Executive Director Andrew Shepherd
Producer Jake Orr
Literary Manager Steve Harper
Operations Manager Anna De Freitas
Marketing Coordinator Jennifer Oliver
Technical Manager Alastair Borland
Literary Associate Lauretta Barrow
Operations Assistant Nyanna Bentham-Prince
Resident Assistant Producers Jessica Moncur, Rhys Newcombe-Jones, Adam Line
Intern Katarina Grabowsky

Theatre503 Board
Erica Whyman (Chair)
Royce Bell (Vice Chair)
Chris Campbell
Joachim Fleury
Celine Gagnon
Eleanor Lloyd
Marcus Markou
Geraldine Sharpe-Newton
Jack Tilbury
Roy Williams OBE

Theatre503 Volunteers
Kelly Agredo, Emma Anderson, Hannah Bates, Emily Brearley-Bayliss, Alex Brent, Debra Dempster, Uju Enendu, Rachel Gemaehling, Ashley Jones, Gareth Jones, Sian Legg, Andre Leonidou, George Linfield, Karen Loewy, Ceri Lothian, Graham McCulloch, Ellen McGahey, Georgia McKnight, Tom Mellors, Camilla Norris, Annabel Pemberton, Lucy Robson, Kate Roche, Sussan Sanii, Kamilah Shorey, Ellie Snow, Paul Sockett, Caroline Summers, Ayaaz Tariq, Thanos Topouzis, Melisa Tehrani, Camilla Walters, Stephanie Withers

OUR SUPPORTERS

We are particularly grateful to Philip and Christine Carne and the long term support of The Carne Trust for our Playwriting Award and 503Five.

Share The Drama Patrons: Angela Hyde-Courtney, Eilene Davidson, Cas & Philip Donald, David Baxter, Erica Whyman, Geraldine Sharpe-Newton, James Bell, Jill Segal, Nick Hern, Marcus Markou, Mike Morfey, Pam Alexander, Patricia Hamzahee, Robert O'Dowd, Rotha Bell, Sean Winnett.

Theatre Refurbishment: Jack Tilbury, Plann, Dynamis, CharcoalBlue, Stage Solutions, Will Bowen, The Theatres Trust

The Foyle Foundation, Arts Council England Grants for the Arts, The Peter Wolff Foundation (503 Production Fund), The Orseis Trust (503Five), Battersea Power Station Foundation (Right to Write) Barbara Broccoli/EON, Wimbledon Community Foundation (Five-O-Fresh), Nick Hern Books (503 Playwriting Award), Wandsworth Borough Council, The Golsonscott Foundation.

Theatre503 is in receipt of funding from Arts Council England's Catalyst: Evolve fund, match funding every pound raised in new income until July 2019.

Dedicated to the memory of sister Razan al-Najjar, and all the innocent victims of tyranny, oppression and murder in every corner of the world.

Razan al-Najjar was a young 21-year-old female Palestinian medic murdered on 1st June 2018 by an Israeli sniper. She was aiding injured protesters in the occupied land of Palestine, Gaza Strip.

I would like to thank Esther Baker, Jennie McClure and all the Synergy family for supporting me on this creative journey.

A special thank you to Neil Grutchfield whose structural and dramatic input was integral to me finalising the play.

I thank my mother Suzan Harmer for her constant love and support.

To my wife Yasmine whose creative support, belief, love and loyalty throughout the good and bad times of life has been unimaginable, thank you.

All praises and thanks to Allah for the endless blessings I receive daily.

Martin Askew

THERE IS A FIELD

OBERON BOOKS
LONDON

WWW.OBERONBOOKS.COM

First published in February 2019 by Oberon Books Ltd
521 Caledonian Road, London N7 9RH
Tel: +44 (0) 20 7607 3637 / Fax: +44 (0) 20 7607 3629
e-mail: info@oberonbooks.com
www.oberonbooks.com

Copyright © Martin Askew 2019. Martin Askew is hereby identified
as author of this play in accordance with section 77 of the Copyright,
Designs and Patents Act 1988. The author has asserted his moral rights.

All rights whatsoever in this play are strictly reserved and application for
performance etc. should be made before commencement of rehearsal
to Synergy Theatre Project, 8, St Thomas St, London, SE1 9RR
(info@synergytheatreproject.co.uk). No performance may be given unless
a licence has been obtained, and no alterations may be made in the title
or the text of the play without the author's prior written consent.

You may not copy, store, distribute, transmit, reproduce or otherwise
make available this publication (or any part of it) in any form, or
binding or by any means (print, electronic, digital, optical, mechanical,
photocopying, recording or otherwise), without the prior written
permission of the publisher.

A catalogue record for this book is available from the British Library.

PB ISBN: 9781786827340
E ISBN: 9781786827357

Cover credit: Lidia Crisafulli & Joel Baker

Printed and bound by 4EDGE Limited, Hockley, Essex, UK.
eBook conversion by Lapiz Digital Services, India.

Visit www.oberonbooks.com to read more about all our books and to buy them. You will
also find features, author interviews and news of any author events, and you can sign up for
e-newsletters so that you're always first to hear about our new releases.

Printed on FSC® accredited paper

10 9 8 7 6 5 4 3 2 1

Characters

ABDULLAH / MARK
28, a White cockney Muslim.

SALEH
28, London born of Moroccan origin.

AMINA
26, British Algerian.

MAUREEN
Late 50s, White.

TONY
26, White.

ACT ONE

SCENE ONE.

January. Dawn, Tuesday morning. Whitechapel centre for the homeless. A homeless VAGRANT lies in a pissy doorway. A dog is with him, beer cans all over the place. ABDULLAH stands in a grey Islamic robe, 28 years old, a white cockney Muslim in all his glory talking to a drunk. Neither of them have noticed SALEH, 28, London born of Moroccan origin, at the side of the road, watching.

ABDULLAH: Let's just say it's a fresh start *(Beat.)* How does that sound feller?

The VAGRANT picks up his worldly belongings to leave.

ABDULLAH: Allah loves you!!

VAGRANT: FUCK OFF!

Exit VAGRANT.

SALEH makes his presence known.

SALEH: Brother Assalam Walaykum.

ABDULLAH: Saleh! Walaykum salam wa rahmatullah.

SALEH: Where you been?

ABDULLAH: I needed to get my head together.

SALEH: It's been six months bruv, you couldn't even send a postcard to your best pal?

ABDULLAH: Your only pal.

SALEH: Fuck off you mug.

ABDULLAH: Don't curse it's not Islamic.

SALEH: Shut up Islamic, what do you know?

ABDULLAH: You ain't changed much.

SALEH: You have. You look like a Sheikh in Mecca bro.

ABDULLAH: This thobe was a gift, a brother brought it back from Hajj.

SALEH: Looks a little bit cold.

ABDULLAH: It's Sunnah, the way of the Prophet peace be upon him.

SALEH: You know you can still wear western clothes?

ABDULLAH: What you here for anyway? You're looking at me like a cozzer.

SALEH: I see Big Jamal down the mosque at Friday prayers. He said he see you down Whitechapel late at night and you looked fucked.

ABDULLAH: That big fat Mummy's boy. These fake pricks, no Islam, no Deen!

SALEH: How are you feeling?

ABDULLAH: I'm alright. I'm finding my way, my path.

SALEH: You don't have to sleep with tramps.

ABDULLAH: You don't pick and choose who you invite to Islam, we can't all sit round Jamal's condo playing X box.

SALEH: Well them days are gone, I got responsibilities nowdays.

ABDULLAH: You never had responsibilities in your life.

SALEH: I have now. I'm going to be a father.

Pause. ABDULLAH looks stunned.

ABDULLAH: You?

SALEH: Yeah.

ABDULLAH: I swear to God…

ABDULLAH smiles to himself, then laughs.

SALEH: What you laughing at? What?

ABDULLAH: I always thought you was a Jaffa cake bruv!

SALEH: I'm a lion! *(Roars.)*

They play fight quick, jab and left hook.

ABDULLAH: Well done son, congratulations!

ABDULLAH holds his hand up and SALEH returns the slap.

ABDULLAH: Your baby is the future, come out tonight gain some spiritual blessing for the kid before it's born. Come with me. Propagate.

SALEH: I can't be giving Dawah. I'm shattered. I got a degree in Geology and I'm working doubles.

ABDULLAH: You should sign on, be free. Propagate the faith.

SALEH: I can propagate Islam working in the dry cleaners.

ABDULLAH: What, while you clean the shit off their trousers? You've become weak. All that singing and dancing at your Sufi mosque.

SALEH: I like a bit of song and dance and Zikar. It's cool.

ABDULLAH: Life is not meant to be cool!!

SALEH: Well I gotta stay upbeat.

ABDULLAH: When Muslims are being slaughtered all over the world?

SALEH: I need a proper job.

ABDULLAH: So what happens when you get the big job? They'll invite you for a beer after work. You'll say no politely but they'll keep on til you run out of excuses. You'll have an orange juice at first, but they'll pester you each week into having a beer, before you know it you'll be at the office party snorting coke off some shitty toilet seat at three in the morning and having hardcore anal sex with

3

a work colleague in a bug-infested hotel in Bayswater, run by a Vietnamese poof called CamCam.

SALEH: Is it? *(Beat.)* What do you know anyway, you've never been to an office party.

ABDULLAH: Boots.

SALEH: Sorry?

ABDULLAH: Boots, Earls court road.

SALEH: What your Saturday job?

ABDULLAH: They set me up.

SALEH: Mark? I need to –

ABDULLAH: I could've made manager.

SALEH: Mark, will you just –

ABDULLAH: It's not Mark any more. It's Abdullah.

SALEH: Oh nice, slave of Allah. Good choice.

ABDULLAH: Jazakallah.

Pause.

SALEH: Listen, Spurs are playing Liverpool Saturday. Come round mine, we can watch the match on sky, have a bite to eat, Amina will make couscous.

ABDULLAH: I'm busy Saturday, market day.

SALEH: But it's Spurs.

ABDULLAH: The love of sport is worldly ignorance. Wasn't it your Sufi Sheikh who told us Muslims should be in the world as though we are strangers or travellers.

SALEH: No that's Hadith, no he said "If it's religion non-stop, you'll leave the faith, and the middle way is the true path to gaining God's mercy."

4

ABDULLAH touches SALEH's western jeans and hooded top in disgust.

ABDULLAH: Middle way? You look like X factor in your skinny generic blue jean culture, following their ignorant ways like some homo fag in a Gay magazine.

SALEH: "Raise your words not voice. It is rain that grows flowers not thunder."

ABDULLAH: I'm not angry, I'm just not going to be spoken to by someone who isn't willing to give up his worldly pleasures for Islam, Allah.

SALEH: So rolling around talking bollocks to vagrants in shit an' pissy hostels is your idea of fun.

ABDULLAH: These streets are my home and the poor are my blanket.

SALEH: You're talking shit bruv. You can go home tonight if you want. You're not poor, you've got family.

ABDULLAH: Family?

SALEH: Life changes bruv. Maureen's in a bad way these days. She wants you back.

ABDULLAH: So you didn't see Big Jamal then?

Pause.

SALEH: Na. Maureen asked me to find you.

ABDULLAH: You running errands for her again? She trying to get me a job, be her little soldier? She couldn't give a toss. All she wants is to brag and gossip about her boys, she'll never leave the village her –

SALEH: It's Larry.

Pause.

ABDULLAH: What?

SALEH: He's been doing nights.

5

ABDULLAH: But he's been retired two years.

SALEH: He's been paying off that new kitchen for Maureen. He was on his way home when it happened.

ABDULLAH: What happened?

SALEH: Last week two Americans, they found him down a side street drinking tea out of his thermos flask in the back of his cab. He said he was just about to go home but they begged him to show em the sights because they missed the tourist bus and were leaving town the next day. You know what Larry was like. He showed them all the sights, Buckingham Palace, Trafalgar Square, London Bridge. They laughed about that one. They were ready to go back to their hotel but he insisted on giving them old school London hospitality and said they had to see where Sherlock Holmes lived. They thought he was real! They said he pulled in to Baker Street and then he grabbed his chest. They thought he was joking at first but the cab rolled up the curb. There was an ambulance parked up by Pret A Manger but he died on the spot. Nothing they could do.

Pause.

ABDULLAH: Are you joking with me?

SALEH: I'm sorry brother, sorry.

ABDULLAH: She forced him back out to work again, didn't she?

SALEH: I dunno. The funeral is Friday week. She just wants you home.

Pause.

ABDULLAH: Was she pissed?

SALEH: Na.

ABDULLAH: You're lying Saleh, she was pissed.

SALEH: You need to go home you do know that don't you?

ABDULLAH: I'm not going home.

SALEH: It's your duty, you gotta bury your father.

ABDULLAH: It ain't my duty. Allah is testing me bruv. He died without dignity watched by two fat Yanks. A proper Kuffar.

SALEH: He was Larry for God's sake, he was your dad.

ABDULLAH: No mate, I'm released.

SALEH: What about Maureen and Tony?

ABDULLAH: Who gives a fuck about Maureen and Tony? She'll be lapping him up now, buying him a new suit for the funeral and he'll be bowing at her feet.

SALEH: You have to grieve. Allah wants you to make peace – for Larry's sake at least.

ABDULLAH: What do you know? He's just a casualty of war. And you, you should be ashamed of yourself.

ABDULLAH exits.

SALEH: *(Shouting after him.)* You're making a big mistake Mark, in this life, and the next!

Lights down.

SCENE TWO

The same day, afternoon. Saleh & Amina's flat. SALEH walks in, he notices AMINA, 26, British Algerian, very attractive and pregnant, she is asleep. He tries not to wake her up. He knocks the TV remote and it crashes to the floor. AMINA's eyes open shark-like. She stares at SALEH who stops in his tracks.

AMINA: Where you been all night?

SALEH: In the shit.

7

AMINA: Please don't swear, the baby can hear.

SALEH: Sorry.

AMINA: I couldn't sleep. I texted, I couldn't even leave a voicemail cos your box was full up. Don't you ever check your messages?

SALEH: I know I should have called you but I got caught up down the homeless shelter –

AMINA: What about me Saleh? Are you gonna be here for the baby?

SALEH: Of course I'm gonna be there. I had to go to morning prayers and then I went to work.

AMINA: You missed the scan.

SALEH: Oh God no. Shit.

AMINA: You. You're neglecting me.

SALEH: I'm so so sorry –

AMINA: In Algiers being pregnant means you're special. Your mum, your sisters, your aunties all look after you. You are not honouring your family Saleh. You best start giving me my Islamic rights!

SALEH: I cook dinner for you, I rub oil on your belly twice a day I do everything for you Amina.

AMINA: You shouldn't have to keep reminding me what a good husband you are for doing the most normal things that any man should do.

SALEH: I'm doing my best.

AMINA: It's not good enough Saleh, you should be here. If this carries on I'm going back home to Algiers. I'm not being left on my own at night.

SALEH: I won't leave you again. It's just all come on top. Maureen's in bits. Larry was her life and her sons aint there. I can't just turn my back.

AMINA: They're not your family. You cannot mend them.

SALEH: I had to find Mark.

AMINA: I thought we were done with Mark, are you saying he's back?

SALEH: Maureen wants him home for the funeral but

AMINA: But what?

SALEH: If only it was Mark. *(Beat.)* No, this is the new improved upgraded version Abdullah who's on a quest to save Whitechapel, then the world.

AMINA: Why who's got to him?

SALEH: No one's got to him. He's seeking penances helping the needy.

AMINA: How do you know? If he's out doing Dawah on the streets he must have a teacher, a Sheikh.

Beat.

SALEH: Do you think so? What like a Sheikh Sheikh?

AMINA: Knowing Mark, he'll be learning online with one of those Google Sheikhs.

SALEH: What kind of Google sheik? What like Abu Bakr al-Baghdadi?

AMINA: *(Laughs.)* Don't be so stupid he's probably just online watching YouTube. Why do you care so much anyway? Do you think he's changed for good now?

SALEH: No, he just don't want to bury his dad.

AMINA: He's gotta bury his dad.

SALEH: I worry you know, he's not sleeping, eating Amina, maybe we should have him stay over to keep an eye on him…

AMINA: No way!!

SALEH: It was just a…

AMINA: NO! I don't want him round here.

SALEH: Yeah but it's Maureen, I don't know what I'm going to say to her.

AMINA: Maybe the truth?

SALEH: She's grieving right now for God's sake!

AMINA embraces SALEH.

AMINA: Maureen loves you, she'll understand.

SALEH pulls away.

SALEH: Oh really? What am I going to say? Hello Maureen, you're ex-junkie son is on a mission from Allah to create a New Muslim Caliphate by converting tramps.

AMINA: Be tactful.

SALEH: She don't know he's a Muslim Amina!

AMINA: Oh.

Pause.

SALEH: You can't explain the complexities of Islamic theology to someone like Maureen she'll be….be….

AMINA: Be what?

SALEH: Bamboozled.

AMINA: Why?

SALEH: She reads Take A Break for God's sake.

AMINA: So, I read Take A Break.

SALEH: If I would've known he was turning into a missionary
–

AMINA: You always open your big mouth.

SALEH: You was the first one to congratulate me when he
converted, you was ecstatic!!

AMINA: I was not!

SALEH: You said I would go to Paradise for converting him.
And then you made lamb couscous and that fantastic
apple Tarte Tatin.

AMINA: I always make lamb couscous on a Friday.

SALEH: What about the Tarte Tatin?

AMINA: What about the Tarte Tatin?

SALEH: The Tarte Tatin proves my innocence.

AMINA: Don't point your finger at me.

SALEH: I'm just clarifying a point.

AMINA: Make your points to your mates then.

SALEH: I never see my mates, I'm always at work.

AMINA: Really?

SALEH: Yes, really.

AMINA: It's always Mark before me isn't it?

SALEH: I swear to Allah I don't put Mark before you but his
Dad just passed over.

AMINA: Well why do I feel invisible then?

SALEH: You're not invisible, you're gorgeous… Ravishing.

AMINA: Liar!

SALEH: Beautiful, amazing –

AMINA: No!

SALEH: A glowing angel princess about to grow new wings, the sort of wings I want to touch and rub.

AMINA: But you don't touch do you?

SALEH: Yes I do, I rub oil on your belly.

AMINA: I'm not a shoulder of lamb Saleh.

SALEH moves in close.

SALEH: I don't want to hurt you and the boy is all.

AMINA: Do you know how I feel right now Saleh, do you?

SALEH: Invisible.

AMINA: No. Right here and now!!

SALEH: Pregnant?

AMINA: No, how I feel, the way I feel.

SALEH: Hormonal?

AMINA: Fat!!! Ugly and fat!

SALEH: Not invisible?

AMINA: No, fat!! I don't feel nothing like a winged angel. I feel more like a Jumbo Jet about to crash!

SALEH: You're not fat Amina, you're a beautifully equipped Learjet with a little extra luggage, waiting to unload onto the tarmac.

AMINA: Why don't you fuck this fat ugly Learjet then?

SALEH: What?

Pause. AMINA is looking frustrated now.

AMINA: Fuck me Saleh!! Fuck me!

SALEH: *(Embarrassed.)* Astaghfirullah, Astaghfirullah!!! Don't talk like this please, the baby can hear.

AMINA: I want to be a woman not a piece of roast lamb. I want to feel sexy again.

SALEH: What do you want me to do then?

AMINA: It's not an order, it's your choice.

SALEH tries to touch AMINA's breast and kiss her neck. AMINA recoils.

Get off me!!!

SALEH: Sorry!

AMINA: It's got to be the right moment.

Pause.

SALEH: Why are we arguing Amina? We love each other, the baby's on it's way and I want to spend more time with you but I'm lucky to be working.

AMINA: You don't have to kill yourself working all hours. We just need to spend more time together.

SALEH: I know. This Saturday we'll go for a meal at that Lebanese restaurant you like on Edgware Road

AMINA: Are you mad? We got rent to pay.

SALEH: It's one night out.

AMINA: It's just weird not working, I've always had my own money.

SALEH: It's alright, everything will be alright. You need to rest now and keep strong.

AMINA: You are saving a bit aren't you?

SALEH: Every penny.

AMINA: Good, because we got so much to get baby and me before birth. Gotta think ahead, plan, save your money up.

SALEH: I don't trust banks.

AMINA: Well we can't waste money on restaurants down Edgware Road anymore. *(Beat.)* You did open the savings account with the five hundred pound didn't you?

SALEH: Yeah course I did.

AMINA: Good.

SALEH: I'm sorry. I want to make more time for you.

SALEH kisses AMINA. He breaks off.

SALEH: You know Maureen will be waiting on me. I'm going to have to help her.

AMINA: I know.

AMINA kisses SALEH. She breaks off.

SALEH: What have I done now?

AMINA: It's just something you said.

SALEH: What did I say?

AMINA: That you didn't want to hurt me and *the boy*.

SALEH: Yes so, I don't.

AMINA: Me and *the girl* Saleh, me and the girl.

SALEH: What?

AMINA: It's a girl Saleh.

AMINA laughs, SALEH laughs too, shaking his head.

SALEH: I always wanted a girl. I want her to look just like you.

Lights down

SCENE THREE

The same evening. An open plan kitchen / front room in a flat in the East End of London. The kitchen has recently been refitted with Italian marble. Stage right Front Room, door to hallway opens inwards upstage right. Two modern brown leather lazy armchairs and a glass and wooden coffee table with magazines underneath. Back wall dominated by a large Ikea shelving unit displaying family photos and holding CDs, records, and Arsenal paraphernalia. Downstage left Kitchen sinks and units against the back wall and a window above the sink. Digital radio on the side. Centre stage left a brand new square oak kitchen table with four chairs. Doilies on the table which is set. A half empty bottle of whiskey sits on the kitchen table. An ostentatious bunch of yellow flowers are crowding a cheap vase.

In the front room is MAUREEN HIGGINS, sat at the kitchen table. Maureen is in her late fifties but looks much older, tough face, worn skin, too much bright red lipstick. She is drinking and smoking. SALEH stands.

SALEH: First time he took us over the Arsenal was a night game. I was thirteen and he made me feel so special, one of the boys. He bought me a programme, I still got it at home. Arsenal three West Ham nil. He treated me better than Mark and Tony put together, Larry had a way to make you feel… Made a real fuss, nothing was too much, that was the man, a gentleman.

MAUREEN: He liked you, admired your academia, always said you was a Brainbox.

SALEH: When we scored he squeezed me. I can still smell his Paco Rabanne. Our drinks went all over the row in front, Larry was in hysterics. Some old boy got drenched and Tony got the blame. Larry held the old boy back.

MAUREEN: Nothing vicious about Larry. Gentle giant wasn't he?

SALEH: Tony wanted to knock the old boy out, swiped his cap off on to the pitch. Nutter even back then.

MAUREEN: Larry hated violence, hated it. Mark did too.

SALEH: The only thing Mark hated was Arsenal. Football was religion for Larry.

MAUREEN: Weird how Mark supported Spurs. They fought like cat and dog every Saturday when they come home.

SALEH: What about Tony? He's about yeah?

MAUREEN: Who, silly bollocks? Like the Scarlet Pimpernel him. Loved up with that Tracy Kemp, she got her claws in. No, they've deserted me boy, they've all left the roost.

SALEH: The girls were always his weakness.

MAUREEN: Tracy Kemp is not a weakness, she's a curse. He's fighting again. The postman's not delivering their mail any more.

SALEH: Why?

MAUREEN: He broke the poor bastard's jaw for delivering a gas bill. I had to go down the depot and see the poor feller. He wanted to get the police involved, I sorted it all though.

SALEH: How Maur?

MAUREEN: How do you think?

SALEH: Tony must owe you a fortune.

MAUREEN: The fucking lies that boy tells. I was lapping him right up round here, I even borrowed him three hundred quid for the new suit, but she's like a drug and now he's gone back. He can't be relied on.

SALEH: Nooooo! That's crazy that is, after all you done Maureen, he's mad. I'd be home here, with you.

MAUREEN: But you know what hurt me most, I found out he went on holiday to Portugal with her, I didn't even know he was gone. He can't handle stress, he's weak.

MAUREEN looking stressed lights a fag

MAUREEN: Do you know how hard it's been without the boys home, Tony's in and out like it's an hotel and not even a phonecall off Mark. I'm a nervous wreck, look at me.

SALEH: They're come home Maur. Have faith.

MAUREEN shakes her head.

MAUREEN: Faith? I lost that years ago, faith? I was always awash, with me selfishness. Larry got all me attention. He was my God.

SALEH: You was never awash in my book, just... well...

MAUREEN: What?

SALEH: A little unique...

MAUREEN: Unique? Such wonderful words, you sound like that Melvin Bragg.

SALEH smiles.

SALEH: What nasal you mean? No I read a lot of poetry Maur, it gets me through the day. I remember when me Mum passed over, I fell in love with Rumi, Keats, Yeats. They help me when I'm stressed.

MAUREEN: How'd you get on then? You swore to God you'd find my Mark.

SALEH: I found him.

MAUREEN: Yeah?

SALEH: Yeah. He's well. Good.

MAUREEN's face lights up.

MAUREEN: Did you tell him about his Dad?

SALEH: Yes, I sort of eased it to him like.

MAUREEN: Did he cry?

Pause.

SALEH: Sort of.

MAUREEN: Sort of?

SALEH: He didn't actually cry, he...

MAUREEN: What?

SALEH: *(Thinking on his feet.)* He was, you know...
  melancholic.

MAUREEN: So he's coming home?

SALEH: Yeah

MAUREEN: When boy? When?

SALEH: Soonish Maur, soon.

MAUREEN: Now don't fuck about with me head son, I'm
  grieving, is he coming home or not.

SALEH: He's reevaluating life a bit. I think the shock of
  Larry's death ain't easy on him.

MAUREEN: You tell him he can reevaluate at home, I need
  him.

SALEH: He's not in the best of shape.

MAUREEN: An' I am?

Pause.

SALEH: He's relapsed.

MAUREEN: I don't care if he's got a needle hanging out of
  him, his old room's waiting for him, it's all done the way
  he likes it.

SALEH: I want him home too, he's me best mate, I do, I really
  want him safe with you Maur.

MAUREEN: Have you got a mobile number? An address for
  me, anything?

SALEH: No address, no mobile, nothing.

MAUREEN: What's he become a tramp then?

SALEH: I think he's lost.

MAUREEN: Look at me skin, me hair's falling everywhere, last
  night I thought I was having an heart attack on the stairs.
  What a time to get lost!

SALEH: Mentally lost you know?

MAUREEN: No, you was with him. You spoke to him. You get him.

They hear the sound of the front door being unlocked and pushed open

TONY: *(Off.)* Mummmmm! Maureeeeeeeen!!You home!! I got us a bit of shopping!! Waitrose!!

TONY, 26, white, broad shoulders, 5'10, a stocky powerhouse, staggers in, five shopping bags in tow, like he's never been away. He doesn't notice SALEH in the corner smiling politely and is straight to putting the shopping away.

MAUREEN: Waitrose? You had a win again?

TONY: No, I thought I'd treat you Mum.

MAUREEN: Give us a cuddle then!

MAUREEN kisses TONY like a little boy. TONY notices SALEH sitting in the corner. He straightens up.

TONY: *(To SALEH.)* Oh. Alright? What you doin' here?

SALEH: Your Mum called me over. You OK? Sorry bout Larry.

Beat.

TONY: Yeah, I am too.

MAUREEN: Saleh's found Mark, he's gonna bring him home safe and sound, aint ya boy?

SALEH: In a way –

TONY: Best lock up your jewellery. I hope he has a bath before Dad's funeral.

MAUREEN: I know it's hard on you boy but now you're here. That's what matters. We'll all get through it together eh?

TONY: Yeah Mum, sure.

SALEH: I said they'd come home didn't I Mrs Higgins?

MAUREEN: Mrs Higgins? Blimey Saleh, you're making me feel ancient boy.

SALEH: Sorry, I didn't mean to offend you.

TONY: Well don't talk then smiler.

MAUREEN: Nothing offends me son, only women who hurt me boys.

TONY: We're fine now Mum, Portugal was great.

MAUREEN: Well? Until the next time I suppose.

TONY: *(To SALEH.)* You took Amina away this year have ya?

SALEH: *(Smiles.)* Course not.

MAUREEN: Yeah, well you're home now anyways and that's all that matters.

TONY: Thanks Mum, thanks.

MAUREEN: Saleh do you wanna stay for some dinner? We got plenty now.

MAUREEN smiles at SALEH.

SALEH: No I best get back, Amina gets worried if I stay out late.

MAUREEN: What's a matter with these woman today, ain't got no back bone in em, have they?

TONY: I'll see you out then eh Sal?

MAUREEN: No he's staying. Don't be under the thumb Saleh, they'll have you running from pillar to post like a headless chicken.

TONY: I think Saleh wants to leave now Mum.

MAUREEN looks at SALEH up and down.

MAUREEN: He's grieving with us, ain't you boy?

TONY: Yeah but Amina needs you home don't she?

SALEH: She does, she does.

MAUREEN: *(To TONY.)* Well she can wait. An hour or so won't hurt and you've loaded us up with Waitrose, shame not to be hospitable.

TONY: But I wanted me bath Mum.

MAUREEN: Alright I'll slip upstairs and run you a Radox, just the way you like it, with the bubbles.

TONY looks embarrassed.

SALEH: Do you always make the bubbles Mrs Higgins?

MAUREEN: He won't bath otherwise, still a big baby ain't you son?

TONY going red now.

TONY: I don't want a bath any more, leave it then eh?

MAUREEN: I just want it all back to normal!

Silence.

SALEH receives a text

SALEH: Sorry, it's Amina. I've gotta be going.

MAUREEN: They don't lay off these woman nowadays.

TONY: Leave off Mum.

MAUREEN: I'm sorry son, I'm all over the place. Why don't you sit in your Dad's chair? He'd want that. It's yours now.

MAUREEN offers the chair to TONY. TONY backs away.

TONY: I'll come over tomorrow eh? Make sure you put the meat away, don't let it go to waste.

TONY slaps SALEH on the forehead.

TONY: Spam. *(Beat.)* Make sure me suit's done.

SALEH: Alright Tone.

TONY exits stage right

MAUREEN: What did I say? I didn't say a word.

Pause.

SALEH: I better go too.

MAUREEN: No no, don't leave me, please, don't go.

SALEH: What can I do to help you Maur?

MAUREEN: Well, I suppose you could come down the funeral parlour with me. Would be a great help that son

SALEH: That might be a bit tricky, what with Amina at home alone an' that…

MAUREEN: …sorry boy, I understand. I didn't mean to stick it on you like that, don't worry about it I'll manage all on me own…

SALEH: No, Maur let me come. I'd like to come.

MAUREEN: Would you? You're one in a million boy.

SALEH: Don't think nothing of it. If there's anything else you know I'm here.

MAUREEN: If only they was as stable as you. You're just like Larry. No wonder he loved ya.

SALEH: I loved him too.

MAUREEN: There is something else. It's a lot to ask but…

SALEH: Anything Maur.

MAUREEN: Would you consider accompanying me in the family car? At Larry's funeral?

SALEH: I dunno Maur, I wouldn't want to cause offence to Tony, he seems very upset of late.

MAUREEN: Bout offence? Isn't it Larry that matters now son?

SALEH: For sure.

MAUREEN: It's the right thing to do. Me, you and Mark in the first car, balls to Tony I don't want him near me if she's coming with him. He can get a cab for all I care now.

SALEH: Alright Maur, but I just don't want to cause any problems on the big day.

MAUREEN: You will be my guest, and Larry's guest too.

SALEH: It would be an honour.

MAUREEN: Oh, I nearly forgot.

SALEH: What's wrong Maur?

MAUREEN presents a gift that she's skilfully wrapped.

MAUREEN: I know it's not born yet but I've knitted a babygrow. I thought it might put the smile back on Amina's face.

SALEH: *(Taking the package.)* It's very thoughtful of you Maur, thank you.

MAUREEN: I would have been over to see her myself but I've been up to me neck.

SALEH: She totally understands Maur.

MAUREEN: *(She grips SALEH's shoulder.)* You see what I have to go through.

SALEH: It's not right.

MAUREEN: You will get me Mark home for me boy? Won't ya? Please.

SALEH stares at MAUREEN with intensity.

SALEH: I promise I'll bring him back for you, I promise.

Lights down

SCENE FOUR

Wednesday. Late afternoon. Dry cleaners. TONY, dressed to kill, is at the counter waiting to be served.

TONY: Come on Sinbad? Liven up, a good looking customer is waiting, I'm not some soppy city bod fresh outta' the square mile, it's Tony boy, I'm a busy man. 'Ere ain't it bout fucking time you give me the VIP service and bit of proper discount? Oi!! Saleh you hear me or what?

SALEH emerges from the back

SALEH: Hello Tone, you alright?

TONY snarls. SALEH grabs the ticket book to serve him.

TONY: Yeah course, you?

SALEH: Working. How can I help you?

TONY: Me clobber done yet?

SALEH: What the grey suit?

TONY: No, the *Armani* suit.

SALEH: Where's your ticket?

TONY: I don't need a ticket do I? We're like family ain't we?

SALEH carefully removes his Armani suit from the rail, opens the plastic up and shows him.

SALEH: This it?

TONY inspects the suit meticulously.

TONY: The stain's still on it.

SALEH: It's blood Tone, we need another go at it.

TONY: It's not blood it's red wine.

SALEH: Your Mum told me you've been fighting again.

TONY: It's red wine!

SALEH: OK, whatever but it won't come out in one dry clean.

TONY: Have another go then smiler.

SALEH: I need your owners risk. *(Beat.)* Cos' it's Armani.

TONY: Yeah, me Mum bought it for me didn't she Saleh, I'm sure shes filled you in on me personal life eh?

SALEH: I take no notice of it Tone.

TONY: Give it another clean then.

SALEH: I'll look after it no worries.

Pause.

TONY: Is he back then? Your mate, the victim. Am I gonna have to go on a little expedition to check for needles in his room?

SALEH: He's not ready to come home yet but he will.

TONY: You're not doing very well are you? Maureen will be ever so disappointed.

SALEH: Well the main thing is that we all do right by her

TONY: Yes Maureen comes first and that's the end of it.

TONY looks around the shop.

TONY: This place is a shithole do you know that? How on earth did a good boy like you end up working in this shit? I thought you was supposed to be ambitious you lot?

SALEH: What lot is that Tone?

TONY: Your lot. Ethnics.

SALEH: It's temporary that's all.

TONY: Shame, all that education hasn't really helped you in life has it?

SALEH: Well I got me degree.

25

TONY: *(Applauds)* Three years of life to end up working in a poxy dry cleaning shop.

SALEH: What do you do for a living then Tone?

TONY: I'm an entrepreneur. I have six holidays a year without fail. My Tracy never goes without. And you see them 'Ampsteads? *(TONY bares his teeth.)* They cost me thirty grand down Harley Street. But enough about me, we're talking about you. Let's talk about your future Saleh, cos all I can see in twenty years from now is you with five kids, a grey Mazda with and a big fat curry gut, four ugly wives screaming at you non-stop, without a fucking hair on your head, and that's when you'll want those three years back you wasted on your soppy degree.

We hear beeping. The dry cleaning machine has finished.

SALEH: Look, I'm sorry about Larry, I loved him, he was a great man, but I gotta unload the machine, some of us unfortunates have got to still work.

TONY leans in on SALEH, holds his shirt, stops him from going.

TONY: Here, why don't you work with me then, seeing as though my mother thinks we are family now, how about it? You could sell a bit of puff here, I'll lay you on. Nice gaff to serve up in a dry cleaners, low key, we can be like the Mafia, be partners.

SALEH: *(Smiling.)* No thanks, I can get laid on back home in Morocco, a lot cheaper than your jank.

TONY's face drops, then he looks serious.

TONY: Well bring us in Carlos. We can do some gringo business, I got contacts, I always place me goods. Come on set us up with a move.

SALEH: You know that aint my game Tone. I'll have the suit done Friday, stains all out, first thing…now I gotta dash…

SALEH returns the suit to the rail.

TONY: 'Ere, you know what my Dad used to say about you.

SALEH: Tone, please.

TONY: No you listen, have a bit of respect.

SALEH: OK, I'm listening.

TONY: After football, when we dropped you off and you run up to your Mum me old man would shake his head and say "Look at that poor bastard, still smiling and he's got no Dad. How lucky you are to have me." We'd watch you scurry along that landing like the little peasant you was in those poxy plimsols. Larry had such expectations for you, nicknamed you Brainbox. He was very disappointed to see you end up in the cleaners.

SALEH: Anything else Tone?

TONY: What day's the Armani ready again?

SALEH: I said Friday.

TONY: *(Moving in aggressively.)* Well I fucking forgot didn't I?!!

SALEH: You don't have to swear.

TONY: Don't get lemon with me alright?

SALEH: I ain't.

TONY makes a sorry face.

TONY: Sorry Sal, it's the stress an all. Me head ain't right of late.

Pause. SALEH thinking hard

SALEH: It's alright Tone, I understand but I got problems too you know.

TONY: Yeah, course you have.

Pause.

SALEH looks around the shop, nervous.

27

SALEH: Look Tone. *(Beat.)* I need to tell you something.

TONY: What?

SALEH: It's about your mum. She wants me to…..

TONY: Come on spit it out.

SALEH: She wants me to sit in the car with her at Larry's funeral.

TONY: The family car?

SALEH: I know you probably think I'm trying to wind you up again, but I'm not, it's all your mum. She wants me there and I respect her so much, so I have no choice but to do what she says…ok?

TONY: Ok. That's ok.

SALEH: Just wanted to clear it with you is all, the last thing I want right now is to cause your mother any problems.

TONY: Very thoughtful that is Saleh, very thoughtful.

SALEH: Now if you'll excuse me I gotta really push on…

TONY grabs SALEH.

TONY: Here mug! Do you honestly think a little clingon like you is sitting next to me and my mother on me Dad's funeral, eh well do you?

SALEH grabs TONY's hands to get off him but TONY grabs tighter.

TONY: Come near the car and I swear on my Dad's grave I'll cut your face off, do you hear me?

SALEH pulls away.

SALEH: I hear ya but I'll have to speak to Maureen, alright?

TONY: No I'm not alright, you're a Paki ponce!

SALEH: Ahhhhhh!

TONY smashes SALEH round the head with a right hook. SALEH goes down in one. TONY smashing and kicking SALEH like a rabid dog, brutal and non-stop. SALEH is knocked out. TONY stands over him and shouts.

TONY: SEE! Mouthy!!! You ain't smiling now are you???

TONY stands triumphant, then gives him one last kick.

Now let's see you get in the family car!!!

TONY goes behind the counter and retrieves his Armani suit.

An' don't worry about the suit, I'll get it cleaned myself.

Lights down

SCENE FIVE

Later, that night. TONY is sitting in Larry's chair with a towelling bath robe on, relaxing but looking very grumpy. He starts flicking the SKY TV channels over and over, irritated.

MAUREEN stands over him concerned.

MAUREEN: What's the matter with you? Come on, spit it out.

TONY: I ain't used to having baths anymore. It feels old-fashioned, sort of lazy.

MAUREEN: Lazy? 'Ere your father wasn't lazy, he loved a Radox bath.

TONY: I think you need a shower now Mum.

MAUREEN: Never!! It's sacred a bath, sacred! That's why knife crime is up, and the bloody wars everywhere. Let alone the terrorism. I guarantee you if they implemented baths the world would be a brighter place.

TONY smiles a little.

TONY: If you say so Mum, if you say so.

Pause.

29

MAUREEN: Well it's put the bloody colour back in your face that's for sure, you've been looking so grey.

TONY: I need more sun. It's always raining round ere.

MAUREEN: Come on then, what is it? Tell your old Mum.

TONY: I messed right up with Tracy. I'm worn out with all the rowing.

MAUREEN: You're not married are you?

TONY: It's more than that bird in Portugal. I just do random stuff, like I walk out of a plane crash and there's not a scratch on me.

MAUREEN: You're a man's man. Don't over-analyse it.

TONY: People just step in me way. They don't understand me. I'm a nice guy Mum.

MAUREEN: You're a lovely guy. It's her, not you.

TONY: I'm not talking about Tracy Mum. I've fucked up again. Don't you understand?

MAUREEN: Course I understand. Just tell me what I gotta do and I'll sort it. I always do.

TONY: I wanna stop. I wanna be a better son.

MAUREEN: You're my best son. You're home aint ya?

TONY: I am and I'm happy for that.

MAUREEN: You are. So stop worrying and try to relax.

TONY: Thanks Mum.

MAUREEN: You boys'll be the death of me. *(Beat.)* You best not let me down.

TONY: I won't. I know me and Mark have had our differences but I'll be staunch on the big day, in the car, whether Mark comes or not, right by your side.

MAUREEN: I know you will son *(Beat.)* And Saleh will too. He knows how to deal with people, he'll be very respectful.

TONY: He's naive.

MAUREEN: He's kind.

TONY: Na, you'd be surprised, don't half jar people, he'll end up stabbed to death one day.

MAUREEN: That's a horrible thing to say Tone, horrible.

TONY: He gives off that silly smile all the time. He needs to get his head out the clouds and liven up.

MAUREEN: He's artistic. If he wasn't with Amina I'd book him a poof.

TONY: Well I don't want him sitting next to me.

MAUREEN: Well I don't want your rubbish at my door but we can't always get what we want.

TONY: He ain't even found Mark has he?

MAUREEN: Yes he has, he has.

TONY: Well he ain't home is he?

MAUREEN: No he ain't. So why don't you go and make sure he comes home? You're his brother.

TONY: I don't have it with smackheads.

MAUREEN: Why can't you just bury the hatchet for your fathers sake?

TONY: He nicked off you, he thieved off Dad, he sold his gold watch. Dad kept it all in but I saw him crumble. He took ten years off his life.

MAUREEN: You're loyal Tony and I'll always love ya for that but if you wanna get on then you're gonnna have to start controlling yourself around Mark. I don't need this agg no more.

TONY: I'm sorry. I haven't always been at me best but I'll make you and Dad proud. I promise.

MAUREEN: Yes you will. And Mark will be clean and tidy and there'll be no attitude from either of you cos Saleh will be there.

TONY: Does he have to?

MAUREEN: Saleh is getting in the family car with us son and I don't want another word said alright?

TONY nods.

TONY: Alright Mum. You always know best don't you?

MAUREEN: Yeah, I do.

ACT TWO

SCENE ONE

Saturday Morning.

ABDULLAH is in the communal hallway outside the front door of Saleh & Amina's flat. AMINA stands in his way in all her pregnant glory.

ABDULLAH is looking at the floor, doesn't want to connect eyes with AMINA.

ABDULLAH: Is your Mahram in, your husband.

AMINA: How are you Mark?

> *Pause. Nothing.*

Sorry to hear about your Dad.

> *Silence, ABDULLAH is not answering. AMINA starts shaking her head in disgust*

Oh it's like that. You don't wanna talk to me now.

> *ABDULLAH is still looking at the floor.*

I'm not an alien, or some street whore, you can look at me, you won't go to hell for that.

> *Pause.*

ABDULLAH: Your Mahram in sister?

AMINA: No, brother!

> *ABDULLAH looks up and their eyes connect for the first time.*

ABDULLAH: He's never out on Saturdays.

AMINA: He's never in!

> *Pause.*

ABDULLAH: Look, it's a private matter, please

AMINA: *(Smiling.)* Please?

ABDULLAH: Yes. Please.

Pause.

AMINA: No.

ABDULLAH grunts.

ABDULLAH: Why are you doing this Amina? Why?

AMINA goes to shut the door. ABDULLAH puts his foot in to stops it. AMINA struggles to close it.

Now calm down come on don't be stupid.

AMINA pulls back.

AMINA: You've got no Adab brother.

SALEH enters from the hallway. He's covered up but there is some bruising on his face.

SALEH: What's going on? Abdullah? Salam Walaykum

AMINA: He is forcing his foot in the door like some common criminal don't salam him!

ABDULLAH: Walaykum salam brother, she's crazy.

AMINA: I'm crazy?

SALEH: Show the brother some respect, it's Abdullah.

AMINA: He has no manners.

ABDULLAH: Don't worry Saleh, she's pregnant.

AMINA: There are no real men anymore.

ABDULLAH: She's got a big mouth bro, if I owned her I'd shackle her. She's like a kuffar bird.

AMINA: No one owns me, and I'm not a bird!

SALEH: Shall we all calm it down, maybe all have some mint tea?

ABDULLAH: I tried to be respectful bro, I just want a private chat, men's talk.

AMINA: What talk? Big men's Jihadi talk!!

SALEH: Shshsh!!!! We'll have MI5 at our bloody door, please.

ABDULLAH: She's dangerous bro, watch her, she'll get us all nicked!

AMINA: I can say Jihad if I like, I can sing it if I want. Jihadi Jihadi Jihadi Jihadi!!!!

SALEH is looking very scared, ABDULLAH is shaking his head in disbelief.

ABDULLAH: You need to keep your mouth shut sister. And cover your ornaments. Look Saleh her clothes are tighter than kuffar women.

AMINA: *(To SALEH.)* Did you hear that?

SALEH: Her clothes are fine. I like her clothes.

ABDULLAH: Your choice bruv. All I want is a private talk that's all.

AMINA: Private talk, shit talk, you're a fake Muslim Mark. Bet you want to act out your frustrations don't you like those fake Muslims who murder commuters and schoolgirls.

ABDULLAH: My brother Hassan says we should be Mujahids, Holy warriors who give up the dunya, the worldly life for Paradise.

SALEH: Who's Hassan?

ABDULLAH: Me brother. He's cool.

SALEH: Why don't you invite him round? I'd like to meet him.

AMINA: What is this a hotel?

ABDULLAH: That could be a little bit difficult right now.

AMINA: What is he dead then?

ABDULLAH: No, we have to talk online cos he is not in the UK.

AMINA: *(Smiling.)* See, we best watch him Saleh, he'll end up a lamb to the slaughter like the rest of the Jihadi boys.

SALEH: Please Amina.

ABDULLAH smiles.

ABDULLAH: I love Hassan, he's like a father to me.

AMINA: You only get one father.

ABDULLAH: Well I've got a new family now. They're not petty or parochial and they don't judge me, they just want to save us.

AMINA: Save yourself Mark. You're British, you're one of us no matter what you believe. We are the same in God's eyes. Love is what matters, love!

The boys look at each other.

ABDULLAH: She's jinned up brother talking like that, she needs exorcism.

SALEH: No bruv, she just needs me at home a bit more.

AMINA: *(To SALEH.)* You're pathetic. You have no idea what I go through.

SALEH: *(Meek.)* Sorry Mina, I'm trying to.

AMINA: Shut up! You're eating chicken cottage from now on. An' what you smiling for Mark? You're no better. Ex-junkie thief, just started praying and now you're a Muslim scholar, mashallah!!

ABDULLAH: Yeah, mashallah!

AMINA: All so pious but your Google Sheikh can't get a passport so he teaches his little converts to hate and kill. And who suffers, does he? No. It's the women, the sisters.

We get abused by every city worker, football thug and builder in the street. My hijab is covered in spit.

SALEH: Were you attacked?

AMINA: Shut up. It's alright for you, you trim your beards and blend in. We stand tall and do you know what? I'll admit it, I feel ashamed to be a Muslim at times. You never back us up because you expect a woman in a hijab to conform with your selfish desires and not our beautiful faith. I wear the hijab and I can't hide. I have to put up with the ignorant van drivers and stupid students who shout "Ninja" and "Jihadi bride". And Mark, Saleh! I forgive them all, because I want to be part of this country no matter what I have to go through.

SALEH: Why don't you just take your hijab off?

AMINA: Why should I? I wear my hijab to please Allah and I'll wear it when I choose. I will not be intimidated.

SALEH and ABDULLAH look around concerned, slightly paranoid. AMINA is near to tears.

SALEH goes to her.

SALEH: Why didn't you tell me?

AMINA pushes him away.

AMINA: Don't touch me! I'm going shopping so you can have your private talk in peace.

AMINA walks off in a big strop. ABDULLAH shakes his head in disgust.

ABDULLAH: Wow! She's definitely jinned up. Disobedient.

SALEH: She's not normally like this.

ABDULLAH is studying SALEH's face.

ABDULLAH: So what happened to your face Saleh? Was it Amina?

SALEH: Don't be stupid, Amina would never hurt me.

ABDULLAH: What was it then?

SALEH: An accident down the cleaners. Tumble dryer fell on me. Amina went crazy, wants me to take them to court.

ABDULLAH shakes his head.

ABDULLAH: Get some dignity back, be with the brothers. It's not good to be around women twenty four seven.

SALEH: The prophet said "the best man is the one who is best to his wife".

ABDULLAH: His wives bro, wives. You can have four.

SALEH: Four, you make it sound like an orgy, it's a serious commitment. You got to treat them equally in every aspect of life bro, four wives, four homes, four cars, four credit cards.

ABDULLAH: Allah provides.

SALEH: Listen, I'm in enough trouble with the one wife because of you. Now are you coming in or what?

ABDULLAH hovers.

ABDULLAH: I can't stay brother. I need a favour.

SALEH: Favour?

ABDULLAH: I wouldn't normally ask, but I'm a bit light…

SALEH: I can do anything but money, anything.

ABDULLAH: Look I swear to Allah I'll pay you back. Soon as my dole money goes in my account.

SALEH: Amina would kill me.

ABDULLAH: Subanallah brother, it's me. I'd never ask if it wasn't important.

SALEH: Amina wants a pram. For the baby.

ABDULLAH: A pram?

SALEH: Yes in John Lewis, a Phil and Ted. It's expensive.

ABDULLAH: Stop appeasing her. I'm a Muslim in need my brother.

SALEH: Things are tight!

ABDULLAH: You're working!

SALEH: I'm struggling!

ABDULLAH: I'm struggling too, for Allah!!!

Pause.

SALEH: How much?

ABDULLAH: Five hundred bills

SALEH: Five hundred? You back on the gear?

ABDULLAH: Wallahi! I'm clean.

SALEH shakes his head.

SALEH: That's all I have in the world right now.

ABDULLAH: I'll give you it back straight away, Inshallah.

(ABDULLAH looks around.) Allah will reward you. *(Beat.)* Do I have to go into detail?

SALEH: Try me I'm all ears bro.

ABDULLAH: We need to help our brother Hassan.

SALEH: You want me to fund terrorism?

ABDULLAH makes a face.

ABDULLAH: What are you on brother? You're worse than UKIP. How did we get on to terrorism?

SALEH: I'm sorry bro. It's just the pressure. What's he like then? Why does he need our help?

ABDULLAH: He's a refugee, from Syria originally.

SALEH: Originally?

ABDULLAH: He was a senior lecturer at the university of Damascus, part of the Assad inner circle, but he spoke out against injustice when one of his students, Zihira, was systematically raped by the guards for fourteen days in Adra prison.

SALEH: Shit.

ABDULLAH: She died and it broke Hassan. He wanted to fight but his wife begged him to leave the country, everyone knew he was a marked man. He left everyone he loved behind bro, can you imagine? He's rolled through four countries, Lebanon, Italy, Germany and France.

SALEH: Where is he now?

ABDULLAH: Paris – pisshole called Porte de la Chapelle. It's a horrible, a crime riddled stop-off full of filth, rats and violence. He is a cultured man. He needs a voice, a platform to speak, educate.

SALEH: That's dark.

ABDULLAH: Not if we can get him over here it ain't, he'll be able to organize, Amnesty international and other organizations would support him, he's known, he's not a nobody bro.

SALEH: When did you last speak to him?

ABDULLAH: Last night, I swore to God I would help, for Allah, I love this man.

SALEH: Alright alright…but how?

ABDULLAH: Look, I been online daily with Hassan, he said a brother, an Algerian security guard at the camp is working with some NGOs. He can help. He knows traffickers. All we have to do is Western Union money over and he can get Hassan on some transport to the UK. It's easy he said,

they do it every two months. But we only have a small
window bro. It needs be now...please

SALEH: I would love to help but the money I have. It's not
even really mine.

ABDULLAH: I'm not asking for me, I'm asking in the name of
Allah.

SALEH: Don't do that to me.

ABDULLAH: Are you a Muslim, or a hypocrite?

Pause.

SALEH: It's only because you asked in the name of Allah.
Otherwise...

ABDULLAH: I know.

SALEH: Wait there.

SALEH exits inside

ABDULLAH: You won't regret this brother. This will get you to
the highest part of Paradise.

SALEH: *(off stage.)* Inshallah.

*ABDULLAH pulls out a mobile phone and starts texting quickly.
He hears SALEH coming back and hides the phone in his pocket.*

Here. It's a loan. I hope it helps.

SALEH hands him the money

I want it back though.

ABDULLAH pockets the money.

ABDULLAH: Jazak Allah Khair, thanks. Jazakallah. I want
the truth now. The marks on your face. How did you get
them?

SALEH: I told you.

ABDULLAH: Yeah, yeah, health and safety at work. Who was it then?

SALEH: *(Anxious.)* Look, I don't want no more trouble.

ABDULLAH: Calm down bruv I'm not a copper.

SALEH: I think it's best I keep my mouth shut.

ABDULLAH: Did Big Jamal do that?

SALEH: No.

ABDULLAH: So someone did do something?

Pause.

ABDULLAH: I can wait here til she comes back and ask her if you like?

SALEH: I bumped into your brother. In my shop.

ABDULLAH: So?

SALEH: His Armani suit was stained.

ABDULLAH: And?

SALEH: We had a little disagreement.

ABDULLAH moves in close to SALEH. He touches his face with his hands, SALEH pulls away a little in pain.

ABDULLAH: He done this to you?

SALEH: Yeah but "the wound is the place the light enters you" it's alright.

ABDULLAH: It's not alright Saleh, he needs to learn. You are my brother, just like Hassan. We don't turn our backs on our brothers.

SALEH: Sometimes we have to.

ABDULLAH: I am a witness to this now brother. I must take action or I'm a hypocrite. You saved me when I was down, you helped Hassan too and now I am obligated to help you to find justice.

SALEH: If you really want to help then go home to your mother.

ABDULLAH: If you don't wanna stand up for yourself I will!

SALEH: Your Mum's just lost Larry.

ABDULLAH: I'm gonna kill that dirty kuffar pig... Wallahi!!

ABDULLAH runs off.

SALEH: *(Calling off.)* Abdullah, Abdullah, it was my fault!! It was me, brother!!!

SALEH is left alone, worried.

Darkness. Lights down.

SCENE TWO

MAUREEN's flat, the same night.

MAUREEN: Do you wan' a bit of dinner boy you look shattered?

SALEH: No thanks, I been eating on the run.

MAUREEN: You're skin an' bone, look at ya. Have a custard tart, bulk you up a bit

SALEH: Thanks Maur.

SALEH devours it.

MAUREEN: You been rushing about after Marky?

SALEH: Yeah.

MAUREEN: You found him then?

SALEH: Yeah, but he's bit different Maur, a bit changed.

Pause, MAUREEN thinking.

MAUREEN: What is he gay?

SALEH: No, he's more like me nowdays.

Pause.

MAUREEN: You gay?

SALEH: No. No one's Gay Maur.

MAUREEN: What then?

SALEH: You know when I was helping Mark in rehab.

MAUREEN: Before he went on the missing?

SALEH: Yeah, we'd go in the garden because the room was horrible and bare, didn't even have a telly.

MAUREEN: Tony had a telly in prison.

SALEH: I know, it was rough. He said "I feel naked off the drugs". He was all fidgety, I wanted to calm him so I tried reciting Keats, Ode to a Nightingale:

"My heart aches and a drowsy numbness pains,
My sense as though of hemlock I had drunk,
Or emptied some dull opiate to the drains."

But he looked blank, dead-eyed. Nothing got through, not even Rumi or Yeats. And then he looked at me all tender and said "I wanna do a prayer".

MAUREEN: Poor thing.

SALEH: After we prayed together he said "That was good that" and he asked me if I could sneak him in a Quran. Two weeks later he wanted me to help him with his Shahada.

MAUREEN: Sha-what?

SALEH: It's a proclamation of faith. Where you become a Muslim.

MAUREEN: But he's Catholic. I had him christened in St Monica's.

SALEH: He's converted. He's a Muslim. After he converted he
left.

MAUREEN: Where'd he go?

SALEH: I don't know. I went back there and they said he
didn't even take his stuff. That was six months ago. First
time I see him is when I went looking for him for you.

Pause MAUREEN pours a drink. Then looks confused.

MAUREEN: So he's Muslim. He's off the drugs. That's a good
thing.

SALEH: He's become very devout Maur, with some new
brothers.

MAUREEN: What brothers? Tony's his brother.

SALEH: Muslim brothers, he talks to them over the internet.
This brother Hassan he's with, Mark told me he was a
lecturer from Damascus university who fled persecution to
live in Paris.

MAUREEN: Slow down, you're losing me son.

SALEH: Sorry it's just I've give Mark five hundred quid to
help Hassan cos he said he was bang in trouble. I needed
that money for Amina's pram, she's gonna go mad if she
finds out, she thinks it's in a savings account.

MAUREEN: You best come clean with her Saleh, you can't lie
to a woman about money.

SALEH: I ain't doing that Maur, she'll kill me, then leave
me. Soon as I give him that money me gut said it was a
mistake.

MAUREEN: Why?

SALEH: I went online and nothing Mark said made sense, so
I asked down the mosque, the internet café, the refugee
centre. And the more I searched the more stupid I felt.
How was I to know Hassan was a ghost.

MAUREEN: What do you mean ghost?

SALEH: He ain't a lecturer Maur, he don't bloody exist in Damascus university, it's been closed for ages, cos of the war.

MAUREEN: So?

SALEH: I spoke to Dr Baki. He was a teacher in Damascus and he's never heard of him.

MAUREEN: Who is this Hassan then?

SALEH: I don't know who he is but Dr Baki said I need to contact the authorities.

MAUREEN: What do you wanna call them for? You've been conned. I bet there's a family of Hassans out there having a whale of a time on your monkey.

SALEH: Amina's right Maur. Whoever he is he's got a hold on Mark. I've never known him to be in love like this. It's dangerous. I think he's being brainwashed.

MAUREEN: You fucking winding me up?

SALEH: These online radicals. They prey on the vulnerable, the unloved, the outsiders.

MAUREEN: My Mark isn't unloved.

SALEH: I don't mean to offend Maur but they pick on converts like Mark, cos' they're like new born babies. All they seem to know is how hard the world's been to them and they are willing to give up everything for true spiritual love, the ultimate end to the pain in a way.

MAUREEN: He was always gullible.

SALEH: They only focus on the violent aspects of Jihad.

Beat.

MAUREEN: Go to Paris then – tell this Hassan to leave my boy alone.

SALEH: There is no Hassan. Mark's lied to me Maur. I'm a complete mug.

SALEH holds his head in his hands.

SALEH: He is me best mate Maur... Me best mate

MAUREEN: Is he tryin' to hurt himself again?

SALEH looks at MAUREEN, he panics.

SALEH: I'll call the fucking police, I'll call em now!

MAUREEN: Don't you dare call the old bill, they'll hang him out to dry, they don't understand boys like Mark.

SALEH: I don't know what to do.

MAUREEN: Let me sort it, I'll phone his Uncle Bobby up, he knows heavy people over South, he'll bosh these groomers about.

SALEH: Maureen!!! You can't bully these people with some small time gangsters. They think they work for God!! They're fighting a Holy war.

MAUREEN: No wars are Holy boy.

SALEH: I know but I think they may be using your son to make one of their political points. They send converts on suicide missions.

MAUREEN: He wouldn't kill himself he has panic attacks.

SALEH: He don't have panic attacks anymore, he believes he is doing the ultimate good! He doesn't drink, he doesn't smoke, he hasn't got a girlfriend, he hates football.

MAUREEN: People change, maybe he's growing up. Bout time if you ask me.

SALEH: He's not coming home Maur. He's not coming to the funeral.

MAUREEN: Why?

47

SALEH: I've been telling you why.

Pause.

MAUREEN: Is that why you told me Mark was back on drugs boy?

SALEH drops his head.

What is this bloody religion? *(Pause.)* Look at the state of your boat. You been fighting?

SALEH: What?

MAUREEN: Pointing fingers at my Marky but your face is like a crushed peach. Are you in a Holy War too?

SALEH: No, Maureen, Islam is peace! Peace!

MAUREEN: Oh shut up I'm not a mug. I've seen life and I know men.

SALEH: Tony done it.

MAUREEN: My Tony?

SALEH: Yeah, cos I said I was going to hold your hand in the front car. He went bonkers.

MAUREEN touches SALEH tenderly.

MAUREEN: You won't go to the police will ya?

SALEH: No.

MAUREEN: What am I missing boy?

SALEH: I told Mark and he went mad. I never seen him like that before, Maur. He's out there looking for him.

MAUREEN: On the warpath?

SALEH looks at MAUREEN with little sheep eyes. Scared. Unsure.

SALEH: I'm sorry for all this Maur at this time, really sorry.

MAUREEN holds SALEH who is breaking up a little bit now.

MAUREEN: Don't be sorry son it's not your fault. We're a strong an resilient bunch us lot. My mum and dad survived the Blitz. What Tony done to you is a liberty. I'm gonna have a word with him.

SALEH: No, it's alright Maur.

MAUREEN: It's not alright. I run this house and I know you're a good boy Saleh. A good Muslim. I know you've done your best. No evil is going to tear my family apart.

SALEH: I've messed up Maur. Maybe it would be best all round if I kept a lower profile. Are you sure you want me at the funeral?

MAUREEN: Nothing is gonna to spoil the day, nothing! Larry always put things right and we're all gonna do the same. For him.

SALEH: I just wanted to help.

MAUREEN kisses him on the head like a mother to a son and holds him close.

Lights down.

SCENE THREE

Saturday Night. TONY is standing outside Tracy Kemp's block of flats a little drunk, a big can of lager in hand, shouting up at her window and losing all dignity.

TONY: We was good, fucking Good, me and you babe… Bonny and Clyde… Bonny and fucking Clyde!!

TONY knocks back his can of lager slumps against the pissy wall, opens a fresh one.

I'm staying here, not going anywhere. Staying forever!

A silhouette dressed in white appears in the distance. TONY drinks on.

Tracy… *(calls out.)* Tracy? Please, please. You know I didn't mean it. It was a one off. Punishing me won't help us.

The figure knocks a bottle over on the street. We hear a cat scream.

Who's that? Trace is that you?

No reply. The figure doesn't move. TONY swigs more booze, he throws the can towards the figure, half full. TONY burps in macho defiance. TONY squints his eyes but he can't yet make out this man.

ABDULLAH: Hello Tone. Been grovelling again?

TONY: You going to a fancy dress party?

ABDULLAH: No it's me new look. Islam's all the rage, haven't you heard?

Beat.

TONY: You remind me of all those white wrongen's when I was in scrubs, scared of Arabs and Blacks so they converted for protection. I used to spit over the landing on the traitors shuffling along on subutext.

ABDULLAH: This ain't Wormwood Scrubs Tone.

TONY: How's the smack life? Still banging away?

ABDULLAH: How's Tracy, still doing tricks?

TONY squares up to ABDULLAH, forcing him to back off.

TONY: I'll open you up like a packet of crisps if you start the sarcasm Gandhi bollocks.

TONY puts his hand in his pocket. Knife ready.

ABDULLAH: Gandhi was a Hindu.

TONY: Gandhi was a mouthy cunt, JUST LIKE YOU!

ABDULLAH: Still got a way with the words.

TONY: You better fucking believe it. So drop my private life out, OK?

50

ABDULLAH: We muslims don't let women dictate to us Tone.

TONY: Really cos I see this documentary's all about how you kill women and children in Syria.

ABDULLAH: They're criminals Tone, just like you.

TONY: I wouldn't hurt women or children.

ABDULLAH: No, you just defraud pensioners out of their life savings don't you bruv.

TONY: We all make mistakes.

ABDULLAH: Did you pay them back then?

TONY scratches his head, in pain.

TONY: Why don't you fucking shut up? Do you think I won't hurt you cos you're my brother?

ABDULLAH: Still full of hate ain't you?

TONY: Dad was right about you.

ABDULLAH: Dad's dead.

TONY: Don't you dare disrespect my old man!!

ABDULLAH: Just your old man was he?

TONY: You put him in an early grave an I'll never forgive you.

ABDULLAH: I don't need your forgiveness, just some closure.

TONY: Closure, you're not in a group of middle class ponces massaging your ego now. Do you think cos you're wearing that white dress I won't stab you to death here and now?

ABDULLAH: I'm wearing this thobe because Muslims wear white when they go to war. God, Allah, has blessed me with the truth and I'm making the hakam and judgement on you!

TONY: Oh, I'm scared. You smell like a poof.

ABDULLAH: I've annointed myself. I'm ready to die for Allah.

TONY: Where is he then? I'd like a chat. I could tell him a few things about you.

ABDULLAH: Allah is great He wouldn't talk to a dirty kuffar criminal!

TONY: Why? He fucking created me didn't he?

ABDULLAH: You think you can do as you please and hurt who you like but there's a price Tone. Just you wait til judgement day. You'll see.

TONY: I won't see cos there is only blackness, death. Nothing!!! But if there is a God I'll tell him to his big face. I'll say 'ere God!! Allah! Jehovah, whatever name you fucking use, I'm Tony boy! An' I ain't going nowhere until you let me know a few facts. Why do you create groups like ISIS who chop people's heads off for fun? And then they murder an' rape women and kids in your name. And why do they put them chillies in the kebabs?

ABDULLAH: You're cursed.

TONY: Just tell me the truth, then I swear I'm all yours, I'll put me head on the concrete five times a day like silly bollocks here. Come on, give me an answer?

TONY is pointing his ear to the sky.

TONY: No, nothing? All quiet up there?

ABDULLAH: No it's not all quiet up there Tone. He can hear every word.

TONY: OK then, might as well wake you from your never-ending slumber and confess me sin while you're about. Where do I start? I've had so much fun. There's the wet sex parties, hard booze an' drugs, the heavy violence, the Spandau Ballet concert, the man I shot dead, the wanking, the old couple I didn't mean to hurt. I confess, but what you giving me in return? *(Turning to ABDULLAH)* Then all of a sudden, after my honest confession your God will appear, all curious, in his own trumpety golden drawl and say "You're alright Tony, you've got a good heart son, in you go, you're through to the next round!!" BOSH! Sound the old harpsichords, open the gates, up in the penthouse suite. And, you know what, I'll look around in paradise and there won't be a fucking Muslim in sight, or a soppy little Jewboy, thick Christians, or farting Hindus, not even a begging Buddhist, not one religious person in the gaff. I'll look up at a silver-lined cloud, and there will be a neon sign reading "All religious cunts now rotting in Hell" I'll smile, like a Cheshire cat, the music will sound up, and me and John Lennon will start singing Imagine. Then I'll live forever in internal bliss. Amen!

ABDULLAH: You cannot be helped.

ABDULLAH turns his back on TONY.

TONY: I can't can I? Look, I know me and you hate each other. Sometimes I don't even think you're my brother. But let's put all the bullshit aside and do one thing for our mother because, at the end of the day, we've both been selfish.

ABDULLAH: Easy for you to say. You and Mum always arm in arm down Old Bond Street, wrapped up in your own being. I wasn't selfish you drove me out.

TONY: We gotta bury our Dad!

ABDULLAH: No, you've gotta bury your Dad.

TONY: Do what?

ABDULLAH: He was a disbeliever an adulterer and a drunk, just like you.

ABDULLAH squares up to TONY. TONY instantly pulls a blade and puts it straight to ABDULLAH's throat.

TONY: My Dad was a good man.

ABDULLAH: In Yemen Muslims wear daggers.

TONY: This aint Yemen.

ABDULLAH: They never pull them unless they're gonna draw blood. And if they don't, it's a sign of cowardice, femininity.

TONY: You calling me a poof, bum-nut?

ABDULLAH: True Muslims are never aggressors but when oppressed we wage war till the death. Brave ain't you, with your penknife.

TONY throws the blade and starts making boxing stances.

TONY: Come on then, come on!! Let's have a straightener. Come on!!!

TRACY: *(Offstage.)* Tone what you shouting for?

TONY: Come on Mark, I'll give you a belting like the good old days!

TRACY: *(Offstage.)* You said you was gonna change.

TONY: Alright, alright, I'm sorry babe. It's just me brother.

TRACY: *(Offstage.)* Come up before the police come.

Whilst TONY is distracted ABDULLAH slips away.

TONY: Really?

TRACY: *(Offstage.)* Yeah just for a bit.

TONY looks around.

TONY: You still 'ere?

Lights down

SCENE FOUR

Sunday morning. Speakers' Corner.

ABDULLAH addresses a sceptical crowd. Over his white thobe he now wears an army jacket and a Palestinian keffiyeh scarf.

ABDULLAH: Ask yourself what you know about ISIS. Who are like no one you would meet in real life? What if they are not Muslims but mercenaries?

ARROGANT HECKLER: We know, not all Muslims are terrorists, but it seems that all terrorists are Muslims!!

ABDULLAH: Well how come all these so called terrorists either get blown up and shot dead, or miraculously escape to Syria across five continents? We never seem to have a body to put up on trial do we?

DRUNK HECKLER: You can't catch a fucking suicide bomber can ya!!

ABDULLAH: The Manchester bombing, the Borough Market attacks, the Charlie Hebdo shootings – they were all state-sponsored inside jobs.

ARROGANT HECKLER: They shot coppers in Paris. Was that an inside job?

ABDULLAH: Yes and it was very convincing until I looked closely. How can a policeman, who is apparently assassinated with a gunshot to the head be shown to leave no trace of blood or brain matter? They were blanks. If you don't believe me look up Crisis Actors on YouTube and you'll see paid Secret Services personnel acting out fake drills.

ANGRY HECKLER: You're insane. Why would they do all that?

ABDULLAH: To win public opinion for their unpopular wars they must first create a problem. So they employ ISIS to be your problem with their barbarism. Then they use the media to manufacture a reaction of fear and paranoia. And finally they offer a solution: our Governments go to war to defend us, save the natives and teach them manners. Problem, reaction, solution.

ANGRY HECKLER: If you don't like it here then why don't you go back home you cunt?

ABDULLAH: This is my home! I'm English, born and bred in the East End of London. My Dad died behind the wheel of his Black cab last week, yeah last week, and for what?

ANGRY HECKLER: Traitor!

ABDULLAH: Traitor? I was a victim in my society, my own family, always on the losing side no matter how hard I worked. But my friend reached out, he reached out to me from a world that was as alien to me as it is to you. And Islam welcomed me. It gave me the strength to stand up against years of oppression and now I'm free.

DRUNK HECKLER: You're on drugs.

ABDULLAH: Yeah, a divine drug. I'm a warrior. Fearless. Craving my end. A warrior is selfless for God and his armour is his blood. Nothing can hurt me.

ANGRY HECKLER: I'll hurt you in a minute.

Laughter

ABDULLAH: Even your anger looks beautiful to me today. I'm a phoenix! You too can be the same, WE can become gloriously powerful together as ONE.

ANGRY HECKLER: What become a fucking Muslim?

ABDULLAH: Your hatred and ugliness is what's stopping you from being free my friend!

LONE MAN: So what's your solution then?

ARROGANT HECKLER: Nuke these dirty bastards off the face of the earth for good!!

ABDULLAH: We need spiritual boundaries to protect our human and civil rights. I pretended to tolerate all religions and behaviours just as long as they didn't infringe on my right to be numbed by TV, drugs and drink. Where did all that tolerance get us?

ANGRY HECKLER: I don't want no Sharia Law, I love our FREEDOM!

ABDULLAH: You're all so concerned about your freedom of speech. What about the millions of people who've lost their lives? Murdered in Palestine, Iraq, Syria, Afghanistan, Pakistan, Somalia, Libya, Chechnya, Algeria, Yemen, Kashmir?

LONE MAN: I was outside Parliament protesting against the Iraq War. We all stood hand in hand. A million of us, Christians, Jews, Muslims, but your type hate all Westerners.

ABDULLAH: We don't hate Westerners we hate your apathy. When they bombed Iraq on a lie the whole democratic world was having THE largest anti-war rally in history. That sort of people power should've created change but it didn't do a thing.

LONE MAN: What's your answer then, friend?

ANGRY HECKLER: He's not our fucking friend he's a traitor, don't sympathize with him he's scum!!

ABDULLAH smiles

ABDULLAH: To believe under one banner of faith, and love God, Allah with all your heart! This cancerous status quo must change, so YOU the decent people can have back God given rights. I ask you here today to open your arms and embrace us, embrace me.

ABDULLAH opens his arms in welcome.

Lights down

SCENE FIVE

Monday, after midday.

The Mosque. Upstage the prayer hall, downstage the forecourt. SALEH is in the prayer hall just finishing prayers, ABDULLAH comes in and stands and prays next to him. They both bow in unison, it's a beautiful moment. They both sit. A wild smile breaks out across ABDULLAH's face.

SALEH: Where you been? What you smiling about?

ABDULLAH: I'm happy, really happy.

SALEH: Why, what you into now?

ABDULLAH: Beautiful things, revolutionary things. I been out on the streets for Allah.

SALEH: Calm down bro, the brothers are all looking over.

ABDULLAH: I converted this guy to Islam. He loves us. The reward I'll gain in Paradise Inshallah!!!

ABDULLAH is getting quite emotional. SALEH is looking round, slightly embarrassed.

SALEH: Come let's talk outside eh?

ABDULLAH holds his hands up to the sky, making a very powerful dua(prayer)

ABDULLAH: Ya Allah!!! Ya Aziz!!! Hear us, our pain, our sorrow

SALEH pulls on ABDULLAH's long Muslim robe.

SALEH: Come on bro, Dr Baki is looking –

ABDULLAH: Give us the strength, thank you Allah!!!!!

SALEH: I'll get barred. Let's go yeah?

ABDULLAH: Why? I'm not doing anything wrong! Hey brothers! Why you all looking at me like that? Eh? You never seen a real Muslim before? Is it cos I'm white? Fakes all of you!

SALEH: Come on mate, let's get some air.

SALEH pulls him out now, with firmness.

ABDULLAH: *(Looking back.)* Yes!!! I'm the real deal brothers!!!
Keep looking at me!! Yes keep looking at me, a real
Muslim!!! Allah Akbar!!!

*SALEH eventually gets him outside. ABDULLAH hugs him, kisses
him, it's weird, he is kissing SALEH's hand, then looks at him,
intent, at his bruises, goes to kiss him again. SALEH pulls away.*

SALEH: What's the matter with you?

ABDULLAH: *(Smiling wildly)* Nothing. I was testing them, to
see how strong they are.

SALEH: You're off your head.

ABDULLAH: I can see the fear in their beady little eyes. More
concerned about their businesses, jobs, and the secular
state they're enslaved in.

SALEH: Yeah but why all the racist shit in there about "is it cos
I'm white"?

ABDULLAH: I'm sick of them looking at me because I ain't
Bangladeshi or Arab like them. It's not sunnah. Its tribal
backwardness.

SALEH: Will you stop all this shit talk?

ABDULLAH: I know you think I'm a bit mad, but I'm not bro,
it's just all making sense to me. Hassan's been teaching me
about pure intention.

SALEH grimaces, he holds ABDULLAH's shoulder.

SALEH: Listen, you're under a lot of stress mate, you're
vulnerable, grieving.

ABDULLAH: Noooo I'm not, I'm really, really not brother!

SALEH: Yes you are!!! I'm worried for you right now, look
Abdullah take my advice, none of us know the truth,

Rumi says "Be silent only the hand of God can remove the burden of the heart". Truth can be subjective.

ABDULLAH: No, it's within your own experiences you find it, I'm telling you, I literally know. I'm living proof of it brother.

Pause

SALEH: What happened to you?

ABDULLAH: When?

SALEH: In the middle of your treatment. You just took off, without telling me? Why?

ABDULLAH: I had this thirst for learning, I couldn't sit about there idle. I wanted to go to a mosque but you was so busy at the time and you helped me so much. *(Beat.)* So I went on me own, asked the kebab guy in the high street where the nearest mosque was and he said across the road. Like it was all meant. Then I walked in, lovely old place, used to be a minicab office. That's when I met our brother Hassan.

SALEH: What, the brother in Paris?

ABDULLAH: He wasn't in Paris then. He was in the wudu area washing his feet, I didn't know what to do... He showed me everything, he was glowing, shining. We prayed together. Then he showed me a photo of his wife and kids, beautiful. He said he'd see them again. Godwilling. And I just knew everything was gonna be alright. He showed me the room he was staying in. Full of fold up chairs and a little sleeping bag on the floor in the corner. He offered me some tea and I unloaded me life story to him, I started to cry....I never cry....you know?

SALEH: You could've come to me.

ABDULLAH's eyes are watering.

ABDULLAH: I know I could've but Hassan touched me so deep I didn't know what to do.

SALEH: What do you mean?

ABDULLAH: I thought his family were alive you see…but they was all dead, they had been murdered by the Syrian Army. I was busy telling him about the East End and all my domestic shit. How pathetic is that eh?

Pause.

ABDULLAH: And he was smiling at me. I couldn't look him in the eyes and he knew, he knew. It was like he could see the shame all over me. And do you know what he done? He hugged me, he fucking hugged me. He said that I shouldn't be on me own, that I needed to be with brothers, Muslims – so I left treatment and I went to live with him.

Beat.

SALEH: So how did he end up in Paris?

ABDULLAH: He got grassed up. Immigration deported him.

SALEH: Did he get the money ok?

ABDULLAH: Yeah, he got the money. Western Union bruv.

SALEH: Why are you lying to me?

ABDULLAH: I'm not, I've got a receipt. Four Hundred and Fifty quid after commission. They're thieves.

SALEH: OK. Let's see the receipt then.

ABDULLAH: *(Makes to search his jacket.)* It aint in this jacket, I must have left it at the hostel.

SALEH: You don't get deported to Paris when you're from Syria bruv. Do you think I'm an imbecile?

ABDULLAH: You think there's rules with the kuffar? They don't care where people die, they just want illegals out.

SALEH: Have you got so little respect for me? Port de la Chapelle was torn down by the French riot police over a year ago. It was in the Telegraph!

ABDULLAH: You can't trust the Zionist media machine bro.

SALEH: There is no Damascus university any more. I looked up their lecturers going back 15 years, not one Hassan. A couple of Husseins but not one Hassan. Is there anything you've told me that isn't a lie? Does this Hassan brother even exist or did you just invent him?

ABDULLAH: Hassan exists and he is the man I met in the mosque. But if I told you the whole story you'd be like the rest of them mugs in there. Wanting to set up direct debits and see two proofs of ID just to make sure they're the right kind of Muslim to help.

SALEH: You can't even see it. You're being groomed. It's written all over your face.

ABDULLAH: I feel like I know how the Prophet Muhammad, peace be upon him, must have felt back in the Golden age.

SALEH: I bet you do.

ABDULLAH: I do, he was pure of intention, clean. He changed the world with his actions, right? Am I right?

SALEH: He didn't react for ten whole years bro.

ABDULLAH: Yes but when he did act, armies came to light, Muslims fought back, Islamic culture spread across the world and the power began to come to him in abundance.

SALEH: You been Muslim ten minutes, not ten years.

ABDULLAH: I made my patience with my family for more than ten years. Once, I would've been torn apart by my Dad's death, yeah? Or by Tony belting you. I would've stuck a needle in my arm to cope.

SALEH: Maybe.

ABDULLAH: No maybe, I would of. But now I love it, the pain, the hate, the rage, but more than that I'm energized by it, it drives me on. Don't you understand what I am saying bruv?

SALEH: No, not really.

ABDULLAH: I laid it all to bed.

SALEH: What have you done?

ABDULLAH: It doesn't matter what I done, it's how my world has changed because of what I done, that's divine.

SALEH: What did you do?

ABDULLAH smiles.

ABDULLAH: I done Tony.

SALEH: You never.

ABDULLAH: He fell like an oak tree. He went down in one hit, like a film. It was amazing!

SALEH: Is he alright?

ABDULLAH: I don't care.

SALEH: I know you don't care. Well is he?

ABDULLAH: He was spark out.

SALEH: Dead?

ABDULLAH: If only. You need to listen to me because I was inspired.

SALEH: How's that then?

ABDULLAH: *(Engrossed)* While he lay there, I just had this urge, it was so impulsive, there was beauty in the ugliness of it believe me.

SALEH: What?

ABDULLAH: I pissed all over him.

63

SALEH: Pissed?

ABDULLAH: All over him. *(Beat.)* All that weight got lifted. It was like the last drop of pain coming out through the end of my cock. He lay there quite beautiful, like a fallen angel, still, motionless, spark out and wet in that illuminating puddle. It's then I knew I had become free.

SALEH: You're off your fucking head.

ABDULLAH smiling insane now. SALEH shaking his head in disgust but ABDULLAH needs to carry on.

ABDULLAH: Then that slapper Tracy pulled on me hair and I came back into the world again, like a sudden birth, into the dunya, the screams, the pain. I pushed her so hard she flew like rag doll on to the curb.

ABDULLAH gleefully smiles in remembrance.

SALEH: And you smile. There is nothing divine about these actions, nothing!

ABDULLAH: He attacked you, It's halal to gain our rights back. I did it for your honour!

SALEH: That's not honour!

ABDULLAH: It's justice then, he had it coming.

SALEH: Bollocks he had it coming, he's your brother.

ABDULLAH: He's history. Ancient history!

SALEH: No, he's a part of me. US! He's you, we all grew up together, loved and laughed together. I was the one who got beat up. You don't represent my rage, my anger. I didn't ask you to go and do a fucking Liam Neeson on him did I? He's your family. You only get one!!

ABDULLAH: Just be happy in the moment Saleh, it's done now.

SALEH: Done? Oh thank you O wise one, thank you for your defence of my honour, thank you.

ABDULLAH: You're going a little bit overboard mate.

SALEH is holding his rage in, he is trying to stay calm.

SALEH: I'm lying to my wife cos of you.

ABDULLAH: You're looking at me like you want to kill me
Saleh. You wanna kill me brother? Are you too scared to
act upon it like a man?

SALEH snarling at ABDULLAH.

SALEH: Your mother was right about ya. You was always
weak.

ABDULLAH: Oh, that's nice.

SALEH: What, you going to piss over me too, eh? You just run
away from everything in your life. And this faith is the
same fix as the drugs were. I wish I never introduced you
to Islam.

ABDULLAH: You don't know what you're talking about.

SALEH: I know you. You're too scared of being ordinary,
being nice to her.

ABDULLAH: To who?

ABDULLAH eyes him, a little taken back.

SALEH: Your mother! Why, couldn't you just try to make her
life a little bit more bearable?

ABDULLAH: Saleh –

SALEH waves a finger in his face.

SALEH: NO SHUT UP! I've had enough of you! I NEED to
let you know what's on my mind.

ABDULLAH: Listen, I done my best.

SALEH: Right now your mother is in the most terrible pain, so
much so she even asked me to get in a funeral car with her
for your own father's burial. She knows you're not man

enough to go back and face it all. Tony may be a slag but the truth is, he's a better son than you by a mile.

ABDULLAH: You're blinded. They're lying to you.

SALEH: Prove it then. Go home and comfort her. Be a son.

ABDULLAH: Do what!

SALEH: You heard me, coward! Facing your mother is your true Jihad. It's alright shouting and screaming about Islam in the streets, telling everyone where they're going wrong but when it comes to real action, not violence, real action, you're a little scared boy.

ABDULLAH: Fuck you.

SALEH: You're just a hollow little hypocrite.

ABDULLAH: You got a big mouth Saleh.

SALEH sniffs at the time on his phone.

SALEH: I want my money back.

SALEH walks off in disgust

ABDULLAH: *(Shouting out after SALEH.)* I done my brother for you!!! I'm no coward!!! Do you hear me Saleh? Do you hear me?

ABDULLAH stands, seems slightly pathetic, small, lost. He looks around, his world's fallen in a little.

Lights down

ACT THREE

SCENE ONE

Early hours, Tuesday morning.

Maureen's flat. MAUREEN is in her dressing gown and fluffy slippers. She's at the kitchen table smoking. LBC on the radio. A knock at the door. She looks at the wall clock. It's 2.38am. She straightens herself up, extinguishes her cigarette. Another knock, more urgent.

MAUREEN: Alright.

She looks through the spy hole.

MAUREEN: Is that you Mark?

MAUREEN opens the door

Hello son.

ABDULLAH is wearing an Italian black suit.

You look good, all suited up… like you're going to a wedding.

ABDULLAH: Yeah well I made an effort an I? Come to see me old mum.

MAUREEN: Old, I'm not old, an' I'm not dead either. Do you wanna cuppa tea cos I'm gasping?

ABDULLAH: No, I'm not staying too long, I've gotta dash. Just a fleeting visit.

MAUREEN studies him

MAUREEN: But you like a cuppa don't you? Eh?

ABDULLAH: I'm fine.

MAUREEN: A sausage sandwich then? Or something? Bitta sponge cake maybe? Or you off that too?

ABDULLAH: No thanks.

MAUREEN: Well come in then.

ABDULLAH carries a small suitcase which he deposits inside by the front door. He stops and looks at his Mum for a second too long.

MAUREEN: You can take it upstairs. Your room's all done.

ABDULLAH: No, it's alright.

MAUREEN: Suit yourself *(Beat.)* The way Saleh was talking was like you've changed. You look like you've been down Saville Row.

ABDULLAH: You know Saleh. Under the thumb aint he?

Beat.

MAUREEN: He was saying you've become a bloody Muslim. I thought you'd have a dress on.

ABDULLAH: No dress, just me.

Pause.

MAUREEN: Well, as long as you're off that shit, who cares if you've gone all soppy.

ABDULLAH: Alhumdallah I'm not soppy.

MAUREEN: Good, bout time too.

Pause.

ABDULLAH: You OK, are you Maur?

MAUREEN: No, not really.

Pause.

ABDULLAH: This kitchen's nice, is it new?

MAUREEN: Your father insisted.

ABDULLAH: Larry's last wish was it?

MAUREEN: I waited a long time.

ABDULLAH: I bet you did.

MAUREEN: It's fucking Ikea.

ABDULLAH turns his nose up. Snarls.

ABDULLAH: Looks like Italian marble to me.

MAUREEN: We cancelled our holiday.

ABDULLAH rubs his hand on the marble

ABDULLAH: Some legacy that.

MAUREEN: You've got a cheek.

ABDULLAH: Yeah but you got a new kitchen.

MAUREEN lights a fag up.

ABDULLAH: I thought you gave up.

MAUREEN: I did. But I kept thinking of you and I started again.

ABDULLAH: You wanna look after yourself mother, it's lonely in them hospices.

MAUREEN: So you're not gonna look after me son, that's a shame.

ABDULLAH: Like you looked after Dad?

MAUREEN: I treated him like a King.

ABDULLAH: So why was he was back out grafting again?

MAUREEN: I nagged that man, day and night to stop working. You know what he was like.

ABDULLAH: No I don't what was he like Maur, I didn't see him did I?

MAUREEN: He just wanted to make everyone safe didn't he?

ABDULLAH: Safe?

MAUREEN: Yeah, financially safe, and secure. Not like when he was a boy, I told him a million bloody times to put his feet up.

ABDULLAH: *(Under his breath.)* Course you did.

MAUREEN: What did you say?

ABDULLAH: Nothing much. *(Beat.)* How's your golden boy then?

MAUREEN: Don't you know? He took a right belting off someone.

ABDULLAH: Really?

MAUREEN: Yeah, Tracy phoned me from the hospital. He didn't know what bloody day it was.

ABDULLAH: You live by the sword –

MAUREEN: Now he's left me and he's parked up round that soppy whore's gaff.

ABDULLAH: Every woman Tony brought home was a whore in your book, Mum.

MAUREEN: Tony doesn't understand women. He's soft. They manipulate him.

ABDULLAH: You bait those girls. You terrify them.

MAUREEN: I've done nothing of the kind.

ABDULLAH: She's got balls though, I'll give her that.

MAUREEN: You've got no idea.

ABDULLAH moves to regard Larry's chair.

ABDULLAH: I'll miss him I will.

MAUREEN: Miss him?

ABDULLAH: Yeah.

MAUREEN: He was your father not a fucking pet. You don't miss a father.

ABDULLAH: Don't start Maureen.

MAUREEN: Where you been eh? He wanted to see ya.

ABDULLAH: I wanted to see him.

MAUREEN: You shoulda come round then.

ABDULLAH: You wouldn't a let me in.

MAUREEN: You was thieving off us.

ABDULLAH: Well, that's all past now. Bad history.

MAUREEN: Stop fucking about with me boy! I've made all the arrangements and I need to walk in that church on Friday with me sons. So everyone can see that our Larry was a good man, not for me for him, and that he looked after us all. I need you beside me for that.

ABDULLAH: You want me home now Mum?

MAUREEN: Yes, I do.

ABDULLAH: Is that why you slung me out on the street then?

MAUREEN: You was sticking needles in your arm!

ABDULLAH: Lucky I had my brothers out there, real family.

MAUREEN: Brothers? They ain't your blood. We're the ones who clothed you, took you hospital, listened to your tantrums. What do they know about you? Your fairweather fucking friends. We were there when it mattered most, US!

ABDULLAH: Us...

MAUREEN goes to the Ikea unit and opens a cigar box. She holds a wad of £50 notes.

MAUREEN: Here! Larry wanted you to have it.

ABDULLAH: Money?

MAUREEN crosses to the kitchen

MAUREEN: He kept it for you, hoping you'd get clean. And you are clean ain't you?

ABDULLAH: Cleaner than a new born baby.

71

MAUREEN: It's yours, your inheritance. He wanted you to have it. *(Beat.)* Now take it.

ABDULLAH stares at it in disbelief.

ABDULLAH: I don't want it.

MAUREEN: It's five grand.

ABDULLAH: I don't care.

MAUREEN: He didn't leave Tony a penny. You gotta have it.

ABDULLAH: Why have I gotta have it Maur?

MAUREEN: Because he loved you, and it's his wish, that's why.

ABDULLAH: You can't bribe me any more.

MAUREEN: Do what? You was never too proud to take it before, when you come here day and night with your fucking hand held out-

ABDULLAH: Go on then.

MAUREEN: Crying like a little wimp cos you wanted a bit of that shit!!! You were an ugly little bastard as a child do you know that? I think your heart was deformed and it made you whimper. You were always in me ear like an infection, whining and demanding at me. That's why your father run away to work every night. You was just constantly there, stuck to us all like a limpet. I thought it'd get better when you went to secondary school but it got fucking worse.

ABDULLAH: I was bullied, I needed your support.

MAUREEN: You was always telling tales like a little Mary Ann! You never knew when to keep your mouth shut and fit in because you thought you was better than everyone else but their parents used to tell me to my face what a weasly little coward you was, and I'd stick up for you like a right mug, even though you made me feel so ashamed.

ABDULLAH: I'm sure you made a difference.

MAUREEN: You never got it did ya? If you'd only listened to us you might have got on in life. You was always gonna be a loser. Do you remember the little brown purse I used to hide at the back of the kitchen drawer?

ABDULLAH: Yeah, I used to love nicking out of that poxy purse.

MAUREEN: You idiot. I left it there for you. I knew you didn't have the bottle to go out thieving like your other drug addict mates. I was keeping you out of the nick. But that wasn't good enough for you was it? You had to take liberties an go through my private stuff. I know you nicked my mothers rings. Probably sold them round some smackheads's gaff for £30. You made me look a fool in front of my husband you parasite.

ABDULLAH: I was ill!

MAUREEN: Always an excuse. Now you got this religion you think you're a man? All I see is the same little boy terrified to bury his own Dad.

ABDULLAH: I ain't burying him mother.

MAUREEN: Do what?

ABDULLAH: I said I ain't burying my father.

MAUREEN: You're my eldest, you gotta bury him. It's tradition.

ABDULLAH: I ain't taking part in your Christian charade.

MAUREEN: But it's your father!

MAUREEN looks hurt, confused.

Where's this coming from eh? Your bloody Islam? Well answer me boy, I'm talking to you!!

ABDULLAH: I don't need to answer you, I don't need to prove anything any more.

MAUREEN: He wanted you home though boy, Larry did! Not me, Larry. You owe him that.

ABDULLAH: You're lying.

MAUREEN: No it's true, he loved you more than anything.

ABDULLAH: And he forced me out into the street.

MAUREEN: He was looking for you Thursday week.

ABDULLAH: Lies, lies!

MAUREEN: He was, he said he chased after you down Whitechapel.

ABDULLAH: The only thing he chased was a pound note.

MAUREEN: It was you wasn't it?

ABDULLAH: Stop it.

MAUREEN: I told him not to bother, that you'd come home with your tail between your legs but he's been looking everywhere for the last few months of his life. He was heartbroken. He felt like a failure as a father, he wasn't strict like me.

ABDULLAH: You're cruel not strict.

MAUREEN: He started to get the chest pains cos' you didn't come back. I couldn't make it right. He went to A and E with the stress.

ABDULLAH: Stop blaming me.

MAUREEN: He died in pain an' alone.

ABDULLAH: I didn't kill him.

MAUREEN: You done a bloody good job.

ABDULLAH: Don't you dare judge me, don't you dare!

Long pause.

MAUREEN: Sit down son… Please.

ABDULLAH: Why?

MAUREEN: Just sit down… I got something to tell you.

ABDULLAH: I ain't burying him, I ain't.

MAUREEN: I know, now can't you just let me speak?

ABDULLAH: Go on then.

MAUREEN: It's about Tony.

ABDULLAH: What's he done now?

MAUREEN: Nothing. Just listen to me. *(Beat.)* He's different from you. You know your Dad had a big heart right? Massive heart and he always meant well didn't he?

ABDULLAH: Spit it out.

MAUREEN: Well, when we got him, Tony… He was innocent, alone… We took him home. He'd had a terrible time, he was anaemic. It broke Larry's heart. He swore to me that he'd never go without. And he didn't. Larry spoilt him rotten, well you know that too well don't you? That's why you feel the way you do, but you're Larry's only son, you're his blood.

ABDULLAH: What are you on about Maureen?

MAUREEN: We adopted Tony.

Pause. Mark's mind racing.

ABDULLAH: So he's… what?

MAUREEN: He's not your blood. I lost me ovaries when you was born, an' Larry thought it best we adopt.

ABDULLAH: So me own family hated me because I wasn't a charity case. Great that. Wonderful.

MAUREEN: We didn't want you to grow up alone, we thought it would help you.

ABDULLAH laughs bitterly.

ABDULLAH: So I've been lied to all me life Maur?

MAUREEN: We thought we was protecting you boy, making your life better.

75

ABDULLAH: What kind of people are you? Why didn't you tell me before?

MAUREEN: We didn't want to damage your mind, you had difficulties.

ABDULLAH holds his head. It's hurting.

ABDULLAH: I can't believe this.

ABDULLAH shakes his head, wanders over towards the money, looks at it. Then picks it up.

ABDULLAH: Lot of money this mother? You sure it's mine?

MAUREEN: Yes, all yours son.

ABDULLAH: Worked hard for it did he?

MAUREEN: Yeah. Didn't stop. Always with his family in mind that man.

ABDULLAH: Family. *(Beat.)* Funny thing is this money it's all shiny and crisp, strange that.

MAUREEN: Nothing strange it's good money. Larry's sweat that is.

ABDULLAH feels the notes, smelling them. He nods.

ABDULLAH: Did you get up early Maur?

MAUREEN: What?

ABDULLAH: Take your passport did you, and your special little bag? Lots of little trips that didn't draw attention in the bank eh?

MAUREEN: It's your inheritance son.

ABDULLAH: Larry would've saved my inheritance little by little, filthy notes from the cab, tucked in a cupboard, old and dishevelled. Like you.

MAUREEN: What did you say?

ABDULLAH: It's your money an it Maureen?

ABDULLAH forces the money in her hand.

MAUREEN: What do you mean?

ABDULLAH: You can't kid a kidda can you?

MAUREEN: How dare you.

ABDULLAH: You can't manipulate me.

MAUREEN: I'm giving you a chance here boy.

ABDULLAH: Bit late for that now Mum innit?

MAUREEN: It doesn't have to be. You're clean now. You can show everyone that you've changed. Prove em all wrong by carrying your Dad out of the church. They won't expect that. They'll admire that.

ABDULLAH: I don't need their admiration. I'm free.

MAUREEN: This is your second chance, can't you see it? If you don't take it you won't get another one.

MAUREEN offers ABDULLAH the money again. ABDULLAH takes it but returns the money to the cigar case and slowly shuts it.

ABDULLAH: I'm not here for your money any more.

Pause. Something's changed. MAUREEN eyes him.

MAUREEN: Well, it's there when you need it.

ABDULLAH: Yeah alright then. Let's bury the hatchet eh?

MAUREEN: Course.

ABDULLAH: Good.

Pause

MAUREEN: I don't want much Mark. Just to see you now and again.

ABDULLAH: Do you want me to hold your hand in the car?

MAUREEN: Would ya?

ABDULLAH: And if I do, will you forgive me all my wrongs?

MAUREEN: Course. It would make me the happiest woman alive.

Pause

ABDULLAH: Shall I put the kettle on then?

MAUREEN: You read my mind.

ABDULLAH doesn't move.

ABDULLAH: Have a nice cup a tea ah? Watch a bit of telly. You still buy the crusty bread don't you Mum?

MAUREEN nods

Knew you would. We can have a big sandwich with cheese and piccalilli. Then I'll check all the plugs and doors and see you upstairs safe and sound, sure to put your radio on nice and low the way you like it. And I'll lay on my own beautiful comfy bed and put a bit of Pink Floyd on and relax, Yeah?

Long pause.

ABDULLAH: Have you ever loved me mother?

MAUREEN: Every day boy.

ABDULLAH hugs her and forcefully kisses her on her forehead once more. ABDULLAH slowly pulls away.

ABDULLAH: Then why don't I believe you.

Lights down

SCENE TWO

Wednesday, late afternoon, the light is dying. Saleh & Amina's flat. SALEH is standing by the window, looking out. AMINA stands behind him and holds his shoulders.

AMINA: The rain's stopping.

SALEH: Even when it stops it rains in this country.

AMINA: It wasn't raining yesterday.

SALEH: Yes it was.

AMINA: It was a very beautiful day in the park.

SALEH: You went the park?

AMINA: Yeah, very sunny.

SALEH: Why didn't you let me know you was in the park?

AMINA: You were laying down. I didn't want to disturb you.

SALEH: You should've woke me up I would of come.

AMINA: You don't sleep at night. You've been sitting in the dark glued to your laptop obsessing about your friend Mark.

SALEH: His name's Abdullah. And he's not my friend any more.

Pause.

AMINA: I felt the baby kick.

SALEH: Where?

AMINA: By that big oak tree, you know, near the pond.

SALEH: What oak tree near the pond?

AMINA: I'd never noticed it before, it's beautiful.

SALEH: It's very isolated by the pond, near those woods. Please don't go on your own again.

AMINA: I would love to have shared that moment with you.

SALEH: I'm sorry. I'm finished with Abdullah now, he can't be helped.

AMINA: It's ok. I was meeting someone.

SALEH: Who?

AMINA: Your Maureen.

SALEH: You met Maureen?

AMINA: I needed to help. After everything that's happened. So I called her. She was very warm, and loving. A little sad. We walked and talked.

SALEH: Walked and talked?

AMINA: Well, until we stopped at the park café and had a cup of tea. Then we talked even more.

SALEH: What did you talk about?

AMINA: You, death, life, Mark, Tony. The money Saleh…

Pause.

AMINA: I know you gave them away, our savings….to Mark

SALEH: I was only trying to, I didn't, I thought I was –

AMINA: Slow down, it's alright. Why didn't you set up the account?

SALEH: I wanted to surprise ya. It was for a pram, a Phil and Ted's, from John Lewis. I was waiting for it to go on offer.

AMINA: It's OK. You've got a good heart. Too good sometimes.

SALEH: I know. I've been a mug. Soon as I'm back to work I'll put every single penny aside for you both, nothing for me, I promise.

AMINA: There's no need now, Maureen gave it back. I was thinking we could have that meal, down Edgware Road, like you said, and save the rest.

SALEH: That's Maureen's money that, she's been bailing him out all her life.

AMINA: I tried to say no but she was so insistent, "Please Amina, please you must" she was so ashamed of what Tony did. I had to take it Saleh.

SALEH: I hate Tony for what he done to me.

AMINA: Yeah, well she was angry about it too but it's Mark who's really upset her.

SALEH: So he slipped home then?

AMINA: He didn't hang around too long by all accounts, don't know what he said but it broke her in two. I've never seen her so vulnerable. I just held on to her. You don't realise how frail she is till you hold her. She cares a lot about you Saleh.

SALEH: She's always been there. Through good and bad.

AMINA: Good and bad I know.

SALEH: I think the world of her but I don't want to sit in a car with that racist prick. I don't know if I can even be in the same room as him.

AMINA: I was jealous of Maureen, silly isn't it. And Mark, Abdullah. I wanted you all to myself.

SALEH: "I have so much of you in my heart,
my love is selfish I cannot breathe without you."

AMINA: I felt you cared for them more than me. I am sorry for that.

SALEH: You don't have to be sorry Amina. You've been right all along.

AMINA: No Saleh, Maureen helped me see. I understand why you got involved with it all. You're a good man Saleh, a strong man, Maureen knows that, that's why she depended on you so much.

SALEH: How do I look him in the eye? I can't pretend any more.

AMINA: You know you're going to sit next to Tony in that car Saleh because it's not in your nature not to…

SALEH: If I get beat up at the funeral, will you do him for me?

AMINA: *(Smiling.)* I'll kick his head in.

SCENE THREE

Thursday evening.

The wake. Maureen's flat. The front door is open and we can hear voices from the balcony outside. MAUREEN is dressed in black & TONY wears smart black trousers and a cardigan. He uses a crutch. They look down on the open coffin centre stage right. The coffin sits on a trestle table.

Larry is laid out in the casket in his 1979 Arsenal shirt signed by Alan Sunderland. A little bit too much make up on his cheeks.

TONY: He looks well done he?

MAUREEN: He's seen better days.

Pause.

TONY: Mum, has he got make up on?

MAUREEN: The undertakers let me put a bit of colour in his cheeks.

TONY: Oh yeah.

SALEH and AMINA walk in. TONY and SALEH connect eyes.

MAUREEN: Hello you two, thanks for coming over. Anything I can get you?

AMINA: No, we're fine Maur.

MAUREEN: Did you inform Saleh about the money Tony sent over?

TONY: Mum –

MAUREEN: I wasn't talking to you.

AMINA: Yeah, thanks Maureen.

MAUREEN: Good. Now, Amina, darling, would you do me the honour of lighting a candle for Larry with me?

AMINA: Of course Maur. Larry was ever such a polite man. I wish I could say the same about all the men in your family.

SALEH: Please Mina, your embarrassing Maureen.

AMINA: No Saleh, I'm embarrassing you.

MAUREEN: What my son done was a complete and utter liberty but he's seen the error of his ways and he's got something very important to say to Saleh. Haven't you Tony?

TONY: *(Recites.)* I am very, very remorseful for what I done…
I shouldn't of acted and spoke to Saleh like I did Amina,
but I have seen the error of my ways. I want to be a
better man, husband, friend. The loss of me Dad has been
overwhelming for me….

TONY looks to MAUREEN, she nods him on.

MAUREEN: Please forgive him Saleh. I'd hate to lose you
both.

AMINA: It's alright Maureen. You're a good woman.

MAUREEN: Oh I don't know about that.

SALEH: In time Maur, in time.

AMINA: *(To MAUREEN.)* It's very mild tomorrow. You won't
need your coat.

SALEH: What's happening tomorrow then Maur?

MAUREEN: The funeral boy.

SALEH: No, I mean, will you still need me?

MAUREEN: He ain't coming.

AMINA: *(Taking MAUREEN's hand.)* I'm ever so sorry Maureen.

SALEH: So it's just…

TONY: It's alright Saleh, I'd really appreciate you being there
with us all mate, you was Larry's favourite.

MAUREEN: *(To AMINA.)* 'Ere before I forget! I've got
something for baby. Do you wanna come and have a little
look?

AMINA: Saleh?

SALEH: Yeah, you go babe.

MAUREEN takes AMINA's arm and leads her out.

MAUREEN: Size of you. It's definitely a boy.

Exit MAUREEN and AMINA.

TONY and SALEH both stare at Larry in the coffin

Silence.

TONY: Looks well dun' he? *(Beat.)* The old man?

SALEH: Yeah… Peaceful… Like he's laying on a beach.

TONY closes his eyes.

TONY: *(Mumbles.)* Please Dad, you're in heaven, hallowed be… You was a good Dad, a funny Dad… Up the gunners. Amen.

SALEH: Was that a prayer?

TONY: Dunno… Maybe, maybe not.

SALEH: Well, it's a start an it?

TONY: Tracy's said it'd help if I opened up like.

SALEH: Tracy's a nice girl, she was a good dancer at school.

Pause.

SALEH: If it wasn't for your Dad passing on, I would of nicked you, I would of.

TONY: Grassed me up?

SALEH: Yeah. *(Beat.)* For sure.

Pause.

TONY: Well I would of deserved it spose. Mug an I?

SALEH stares TONY straight in the eye.

SALEH: Why did you belt me like that?

TONY: Done know. Stress, Tracy, me Dad. It's been like a tidal wave of emotions this grief, just sent me off me nut Sal.

SALEH: You Cunt!

Pause.

84

TONY: Yeah, but I'm a good looking cunt an I eh?

TONY holds out a hand for a shake. SALEH looks him up and down

SALEH: You been tryin' a ski again Tone?

TONY: Yeah, same resort as you Sal.

SALEH: You're mad do you know that?

TONY: Life innit? All the years I've been trying to put a ring on Tracy's finger, and nothing. I take one poxy belting, and it's like a miracle, she falls bang in turtle with me. Loves me. Mark should've belted me years ago. I might of been happily married now with three kids. *(Beat.)* I've set a date you know.

SALEH: What? You're getting married?

TONY: Yeah, she's finally banging me up.

SALEH: You best get a job then. Ernest Jones need security.

TONY: Now now, Cheeky! Oh here they come Sal, the gruesome twosome!

MAUREEN and AMINA walk over.

MAUREEN: Nice to see you aint holding no grudges boys, life's too short. Anyway, enough of that bout time we took our places hey… Put a bit of life back in the room.

MAUREEN walks over to the coffin, looks down at Larry. The others join her.

Come on then Tone, let's lighten the mood eh?

TONY: Oh you wanna do it now?

SALEH: Do what?

MAUREEN: His song Saleh. You know.

They smile. AMINA holds SALEH's arm. He looks at her. Smiles.

TONY: Come on then gang, let's have it! A one, a two, a one two three four –

You're everywhere and nowhere baby –
That's where you're at,

(To SALEH.) Going down a bumpy hillside,

SALEH: Hillside

TONY: In your / hippy hat.

MAUREEN: Hippy hat.

TONY & MAUREEN:Flying across the country,
  and getting fat.
  Saying everything is groovy,
  when your tyres are flat
  And it's

ALL: Hi ho silver lining,
  anywhere you go now baby
  I see your sun is shining,
  But I won't make a fuss, though it's obvious

As they continue MAUREEN leans down and kisses Larry. Then stands up and carries on singing

ALL: And it's hi ho silver lining,
  anywhere you go now baby
  I see your sun is shining,
  but I won't make a fuss, though it's obvious

Lights down

SCENE FOUR

Saturday morning. Liverpool Street Station. ABDULLAH sits with his suitcase. SALEH approaches, agitated.

ABDULLAH: *(Stands.)* Salam Walaykum.

SALEH: What do you want?

ABDULLAH: Like that eh?

Pause.

ABDULLAH: You still angry with me?

SALEH: Amina is on her own.

ABDULLAH: I'm sorry, don't judge me.

SALEH: I will judge you, you've given up on your own mother for some charlatan.

ABDULLAH: I'm free now.

SALEH: She was devastated you wasn't at the funeral, you was missed. Deeply missed.

ABDULLAH: I went to see her didn't I, I told her I wasn't going and that's all that matters.

SALEH: She said you an' her had a massive row.

ABDULLAH: She'll survive.

SALEH: She's terrified of losing you.

ABDULLAH: Leave off. I got a train to catch. I brought your money.

ABDULLAH goes to hand some money to SALEH.

SALEH: I don't want it.

ABDULLAH: I don't want be in debt to you.

SALEH: It's not important any more. It's been sorted.

ABDULLAH: You got a kid on the way. Just take it.

SALEH: I was gonna phone the police you know.

ABDULLAH: You should've, they could've deported me too.

SALEH: You was acting crazy.

ABDULLAH: Look, I know I was out of order with my Tony. I just want you to know it wasn't anything to do with you, ok?

SALEH: You said you would avenge my rights. It had everything to do with me.

ABDULLAH: You don't understand. I found love. Pure love without any strings.

SALEH: No I don't understand.

ABDULLAH: You give yourself to everyone and everything. Your poets, your wife, my Mum. You've got nothing left for Allah.

SALEH: Giving myself to people lets me know God. I've been hurt, humiliated and scared. But what I see in your eyes terrifies me Mark.

ABDULLAH: Mark's dead.

SALEH: Look, I know what you want to find, you and your Hassans, but it's trickery brother, they're playing with your mind.

ABDULLAH: You still think I'm some stupid Jihadi don't you?

SALEH: Yes, I do.

ABDULLAH shakes his head.

ABDULLAH: I've found myself, can't you see? Can't you see it on my face?

SALEH: Na, You're violent now, you crossed the line, you was never violent before.

ABDULLAH: I was inside, it was killing me bro.

SALEH: You hate us all don't ya?

ABDULLAH: Na, I love.

SALEH: You never turned up at your fathers funeral for fucksake!!!

Pause.

ABDULLAH: I'm not a bad man. I just want some peace.

SALEH: You need help.

ABDULLAH: Come with me, come.

SALEH: Run away you mean?

ABDULLAH: I'm not running anymore. I just wanna make some choices is all. Like my mother and father did.

SALEH: Why do you need to leave every time it gets rough?

ABDULLAH: You can join me Saleh, you might not be ready now but you can come any time you wish.

SALEH: No. Let's speak with people who know our faith. We can have a bite to eat like the first days, a nice Turkish tea, we can do Zikar, you loved Zikar.

ABDULLAH: The singing's over. My heartbeats are prayers now.

SALEH: We can pray together like before, have that little bit of serenity again. How's that sound brother? Mark? Abdullah?

ABDULLAH holds SALEH, looks into his eyes.

ABDULLAH: My paths been set and it's far away from here I know, my Zikar is constant like fresh air, my story already gleams in the blazing sun, it's real, it's true love Saleh.

SALEH: I know you want to help but the sun will hate your white skin.

ABDULLAH: I don't care about mockers and haters, I know I'm going to do great things, standing up against tyranny is better than a thousand prayers.

SALEH: You won't be needed.

ABDULLAH: This society is corrupted. It has nothing for good people. The Tonys and the Maureens of this world will never understand love.

SALEH: What about me? Am I corrupted?

ABDULLAH: Na, you're full of love. It will fuel me on my journey.

SALEH: You can't leave us all.

Long pause.

ABDULLAH pulls out Larry's cab badge from his pocket.

ABDULLAH: I want you to have this

SALEH: What's that?

ABDULLAH: It's my fathers badge, his hackney cab badge. Maureen will be looking for it. *(Beat.)* Well, I want you to give it to her, from me.

SALEH: Why don't you give it to her?

ABDULLAH holds SALEH, looks into his eyes.

ABDULLAH: I can't do that.

SALEH looks at the badge, smiles.

SALEH: You was at the funeral then?

ABDULLAH: No, I was in the morgue.

SALEH: What?

ABDULLAH: I wanted to do something personal for me Dad.

SALEH: Oh, so you nicked his badge off him.

Beat.

ABDULLAH: I washed him.

SALEH: What, like we do?

ABDULLAH: Yeah, washed him like a Muslim.

SALEH: And they let ya?

ABDULLAH: I said to the gentleman at the funeral parlour "Can I be alone with me Dad?" He said "Course you can, sir". Then I crept in and I never seen him look so still.

I leant down and picked me Dad's arm up, it was ever so light, all fragile an cold, thin, almost see-through, like he'd already faded you know, just a shell.

ABDULLAH's eyes water a little.

ABDULLAH: I washed his face first, then between his hands, arms, legs and feet. Then I kissed him Saleh, I never kissed him when he was alive. He smelt pure and I knew he loved me. Then I prayed for him. And it felt good, like he was alive but in a better place.

SALEH: Paradise bro.

ABDULLAH: I'll miss him.

ABDULLAH starts to cry. SALEH holds him.

SALEH: He did love ya.

ABDULLAH cries. He slowly comes around.

ABDULLAH: I'm sorry bout all this, the stress an that, you know...

SALEH: It's alright bruv, I'm here for ya.

ABDULLAH releases himself

ABDULLAH: I need to go now. Will you please take what I owe you?

ABDULLAH presents the money again, SALEH takes it.

SALEH: I'll pray for you to come back.

ABDULLAH puts his hand out for one last hand shake.

ABDULLAH: Salam Walaykum...

SALEH: Walaykum Salam wa rahmatullah.

SALEH shakes ABDULLAH's hand.

They pull away from each other, ABDULLAH goes to leave.

ABDULLAH: I'd best be off then.

SALEH: Wait.

ABDULLAH: Brother?

SALEH: When you get to *(Beat.)* wherever it is that you're going, can you hold on to some words for me, please.

ABDULLAH: Course. What words?

SALEH: "Out beyond ideas of wrong doing and right doing, There is a field. I'll meet you there."

ABDULLAH: "When the soul lies down in that grass. The world is too full to talk about".

SALEH: You remembered.

ABDULLAH: I was listening, even when I wasn't all there.

SALEH: I thought you was oblivious.

ABDULLAH: Not with you. Never.

SALEH: I'll pray for you to come back.

ABDULLAH: Inshallah.

Exit ABDULLAH.

SALEH: I'll meet you there brother.

Lights down.

THE END